The New Organic Grower's

FOUR-SEASON Harvest

SHERIDAN COUNTY LIBRARY
100 West Laurel Avenue
Plentywood, Montana 59254
(406) 765-2317

The New Organic Grower's

FOUR-SEASON HARVEST

*How to Harvest Fresh Organic Vegetables from
Your Home Garden All Year Long*

ELIOT COLEMAN

*Illustrations by Kathy Bray
Foreword by Barbara Damrosch*

CHELSEA GREEN PUBLISHING COMPANY
POST MILLS, VERMONT

Four-Season Harvest was designed by Ann Aspell.
The typeface is Adobe Garamond. It was printed by
R. R. Donnelley & Sons.

27730   5/18/93   17.95   Ingram

Printed in the United States of America

1 2 3 4 5 6 7 8 9 10

Chelsea Green Publishing Company
PO Box 130, Route 113
Post Mills, Vermont
05058-0130

Library of Congress Cataloguing-in-Publication Data
Coleman, Eliot, 1938-
    The new organic grower's four-season harvest : how to harvest fresh organic
    vegetables from your home garden all year long / Eliot Coleman.
        p.   cm.
    Includes bibliographical references and index.
    ISBN 0-930031-57-1 : $17.95
    1. Vegetable gardening. 2. Organic gardening. I.Title.
    II. Title: Four-season harvest.
    SB324.3.C66 1992
    635.0484—dc20   92-19580
                                                                    CIP

To Ian, Clara, and Melissa,
who enjoy good food.

CONTENTS

List of Tables

PREFACE

This book is a product of three forces—inspiration, improvement, and impetus.

The inspiration came from seeing Scott and Helen Nearing's garden in the late 1960s. Their garden was my first exposure to the possibilities of extending a homegrown harvest. They were producing many crops beyond the typical growing season in the protection of a simple, lean-to greenhouse built into a stone wall.

The improvement came with my experience. Over time I learned to extend both the length of the harvest season and the number of crops grown. The qualities that have always served me well in the garden, informed hunches, stubbornness, and a bias toward low-tech solutions, helped create the productive system described in this book.

The impetus came from my friend Joan Gussow, a nutritionist who has investigated both the potential and the benefits of regional food production. A few years ago during lunch at an agricultural conference, I told her about my success with harvesting fresh vegetables all year-round, even in the chilly climate of New England. She encouraged me to write a book about it. And so I did.

FOREWORD

*I*t's hard to achieve anything new in an endeavor as old as gardening, but Eliot Coleman has done it. After years of experimentation, he has reinvented the gardening year. The old seasons, and the iconography by which we know them, may soon be folklore.

Spring: A mischevious sprite, a warm breeze that moved housebound gardeners out of doors to happily waste themselves, despite whatever mercurial weather tested their commitment. Summer: A Rubenesque goddess who swelled the garden with far more bounty than anyone could tend, let alone eat, even with the help of rabbits and bugs. Fall: A scolding harpy who recited gardeners' failures to them as they picked their way through weeds and sprawling vines to glean tomatoes and squash before the apocalypse of frost. Winter: A wraith who hovered over what was once the garden, whispering, "Gone, gone. . . . Return to your VCR and supermarket vegetables."

Imagine, instead, a scenario in which spring work begins more gradually, summer spares time for other outdoor pleasures, fall is a gearing-up rather than a giving-up, and winter, best of all, is a time to reap a fresh harvest with almost no work. For most of us, "eating out of the garden" is a short seasonal pleasure, unless we live in a very warm place or can afford a heated greenhouse, and the canning-freezing-drying scramble never quite compensates for summer's loss.

The Four-Season Harvest presents a way to eat the best

food—garden-fresh and chemical-free—all year long, with little effort or expense. Most dedicated gardeners know some season-extending techniques, but this book is not merely about season extension. It's about gardening and eating in a manner appropriate to each season.

I first learned something of Eliot's gardening methods through his first book, *The New Organic Grower*. It was refreshing to read someone for whom gardening is not a gladiatorial contest. Eliot makes nature his ally. Because his approach is biological, he focuses on plants and soil rather than high-tech structures. His tools are simple, refined to simpler, perfected as simplest.

Being a simpler-is-better sort of person myself, I was curious to see what Eliot was doing in his own garden, so on a trip to Maine to see my family, I paid him a visit. What I saw was a splendid, productive garden—the end result of twenty-five years of tinkering. Eliot's techniques may have been derived from age-old practices, but they had been recombined, customized, and updated with modern know-how and, occasionally, modern materials. Nothing there was faddish. Just good, logical stuff: a more efficient cold frame; compost made in straw bale containers; subtly redesigned hand tools.

When I questioned Eliot it was obvious that his garden was not the result of his knowledge, but vice versa. He had paid attention to natural systems and they had taught him how to work with nature. This experience gave him enormous confidence in the natural world—the very thing so many gardeners seem to lack.

It became clear to me that Eliot's approach made his life a lot easier. I could see this in the project that was consuming him at the time: the practice of a year-round harvest which he shares in this book. Instead of trying to prolong his summer harvest, Eliot was growing a wide range of cold-tolerant crops (including some I'd never heard of) and then giving them the minimum protection they needed. He was doing this by taking the best cold-protection devices, modifying and recombining them into a system that enabled him to eat homegrown vegetables each day, a system that was inexpensive, easy to maintain, and fun.

Eliot's garden was a beckoning sort of place and he seemed to take constant delight in everything he did there. No wonder he wanted a garden that was "in" all the time, not just half the year.

I left Maine that summer with all sorts of good ideas, eager to try some of them in my Connecticut garden. That never happened. Soon after our meeting, I moved to Maine, and within a year Eliot and I were married. His garden is now "our" garden, though I am only vice president when it comes to the vegetables (he is vice president of the flowers). I can now attest to the joy and ease of eating a fresh, healthy, year-round harvest.

Should you take my word for it? Absolutely not. You'll need to try it for yourself. This book will start you off and steer you in the right direction.

Barbara Damrosch

Harborside, Maine
May 1992

CHAPTER 1

INTRODUCING THE FOUR-SEASON HARVEST

y idea of paradise is a place where I can eat garden-fresh food year-round. I enjoy good food, and I know the vegetables from my home garden taste better and are more nutritious than anything I can buy. Yet I have no desire to move to the tropics or to cover my property with a geodesic dome. Nor can I afford the financial expense and time commitment of a sophisticated greenhouse. Thus, many years ago, I began looking for simple ways to harvest my own vegetables year-round in New England, where I live. To my delight, I discovered that a four-season harvest is simplicity itself.

In the garden, I always try to refine the practice of vegetable culture down to its purest essentials. My goal is the one expressed by Antoine de Saint Exupéry: "Perfection is finally attained not when there is no longer anything to add, but when there is no longer anything to take away." Harmony and simplicity now extend to my food supply. When I harvest fresh vegetables from my garden every day, I eliminate complications. I avoid the effort and frustration of canning and freezing. I avoid the dubious quality and nutrient loss of winter produce that has been transported long distances. I avoid the energy use and technical intricacy of heated greenhouses. It seems almost too good to be true.

The four-season harvest is based on a simple premise. Whereas the *growing season* may be chiefly limited to the warmer months, the *harvest season* has no such limits. I enjoy a year-round harvest by following two practices: *succession planting* and *crop protection.* Succession planting means sowing vegetables more than once (see Chapter 3). Sowings at 2- to 3-week intervals during the growing season will extend the fresh harvest of summer crops for as long as possible. Midsummer to late-summer sowings of hardy crops begin the transition to the cool months. That is where crop protection takes over.

Crop protection means vegetables under cover. The traditional winter vegetables are very hardy. They will survive the fiercest cold under a blanket of snow. Since I can't count on snow cover, I substitute simple protective structures such as cold frames and plastic-covered tunnels. Many delicious winter vegetables need only minimal protection to yield all winter. Thus, in the middle of January, in Maine where winter temperatures dip to -20°F, I can harvest 18 to 20 fresh vegetables from my protected garden (see Chapter 4). All it takes are seeds of some familiar and unfamiliar hardy vegetables, a little crop protection, and a dose of innovative thinking.

The innovative thinking involves realizing that only the harvest season, and not the growing season, needs to be extended. The distinction is important because the harvest season can be extended with cool-weather vegetables and simple crop protection. Extending the growing season, however, involves adding or collecting heat, storing heat, adding insulation to protect that heat, and providing extra lighting to supplement the low winter sun. Growing season extension is highly technological. Harvest season extension is basically biological. It is also just plain logical. The harvest is what you eat.

Year-round, fresh harvesting makes life simpler and easier in a number of ways. Since most of the fall, winter, and spring crops are planted in midsummer to late summer in spaces vacated by summer crops, this system results in year-round eating without year-round gardening. By extending the harvest, you also spread out the work. All the planting doesn't have to be done at once in the spring, and all the harvesting isn't crowded into the late summer. Instead of being a series of chores (putting in the garden, weeding the garden, harvesting, and canning and freezing) with rather rigid time frames, home food production becomes a part of the whole year. The four-season gardener doesn't have a date, such as Memorial Day (traditional in New England), to put in the garden. That's because there is no goal called "putting in the garden." The garden is in all the time. The goal is to eat well.

Is this more time-consuming? Not at all. It is certainly more pleasurable. The four-season harvest is a different arrangement of time and a different appreciation of the importance of quality food. It will free you from the chores of food preservation and trips to the market. You will always have fresh food in the garden—crisp and delicious. You will have set up a system that features many different vegetables in their respective seasons rather than a limited list of vegetables suitable only for the summer season. I suspect that the amount of work comes out the same over the course of the year. The benefits are that the joys of a fresh harvest continue through all four seasons and the food is more nutritious and varied.

If this is such a great idea, why isn't everyone doing it? In many people's minds, the task of supplying most of their food is a large, complicated chore outside of their experience. But the truth is that growing food is the most basic activity of human civilization, not some mysterious industrial process. You do not need a large-scale operation. Your food will be produced in bits and pieces around the year. You will be integrating the garden into your life the way you integrate other important activities, such as helping your children with homework, playing catch and talking with them, sharing in household chores, and helping out the neighbors. You don't hire others to do those jobs. You do them yourself because they are meaningful, joyful, and important to your family's spiritual welfare. Your food is of no less importance.

Getting Started

How do you begin? You can start on an area no larger than a tablecloth. Plant one or two short rows of a few salad crops. Then next week, plant a few more short rows of other crops. Now you're rolling. Less than a month after initiating the process, you will be eating radishes. There are also the early thinnings of spinach, beets, lettuce, and cabbage to add to your salads. Since you will plant many crops in succession, there will be plenty of thinnings. But since you are gardening for the table, there is no chore called "thinning the seedlings." There is only a sequence whereby you thin enough to add to a salad today, thin more for a stir-fry tomorrow, and thin yet again for soup the next day. The act of thinning not only feeds you but also enables future bounty by providing more room for the remaining plants.

As each crop stops producing, you clean off the area and replant it with another vegetable suited to the advancing season. Thus, the warm-weather plantings are replaced by more cold-tolerant varieties and eventually by hardy winter crops. The vegetables for fresh winter eating and the earliest spring sowings are protected by cold frames. Wintered-over crops and outdoor spring sowings pick up the process in spring. (See the specific tables in Chapters 5 and 6.)

Once the year-round harvest has begun to flow, the productivity is unbelievable. Let's say you want fresh salads every day from your garden. There are about two dozen popular salad crops, all of them easily grown in the home garden. Some, such as tomatoes, cucumbers, peppers, and New Zealand spinach, are limited to the warm months. Others, such as lettuce, beets, cabbage, scallions, and Swiss chard, are spring, summer, and fall crops. Spinach, radishes, kohlrabi, mizuna, and peas do best in the cool months. Mâche, sorrel, arugula, escarole, endive, chicory, and claytonia will feed you daily from the winter cold frame even in the coldest climates. Carrots, parsley, onions, and chives can be harvested almost year-round. The edges of those categories will overlap depending on your climatic zone, but the message is clear: year-round fresh salads offer all the variety anyone could want.

If you don't have the space for that impressive salad bar lineup, how about growing your salad mixed? You can sow lettuce and other salad greens together, as in the popular *mesclun* combinations (from a French Provençal word indicating a combination of many ingredients). With mesclun, you harvest the leaves young on a cut-and-come-again basis to make a ready-mixed salad. This is a wonderful option for those who have less time and space to garden and wish to get more variety from each planting. Since the different mesclun mixes are adaptable to a wide range of temperatures and maturity dates, they will yield fresh salads over a good portion of the year from half a dozen succession sowings.

Celebrating Variety and Seasonality

Not only is there a progression from one crop to another, but there is also a progression within crops. Beets become more than beets. They are appreciated as thinnings for a salad, young greens for steaming, baby beets for a cold summer borscht, and eventually large beets for pickling and winter storage. A multi-use pea, such as the sugar snap type, can be used as snow peas when young, as snap peas when mature, and shelled for green peas in between. Since short rows of many crops can be planted successively during their season, the process also repeats itself, like the singing of a round.

Just as I treasure seasonal moments of the year—the first spring rose, a warm summer swim, a crisp fall afternoon, a snow-covered winter landscape—I also treasure the seasonality of the vegetables. I love corn on the cob in midsummer and Belgian endive in midwinter. To every vegetable there is a season if you want it at its best. Recently many of the traditional European cool-season crops, such as mâche, radicchio, Belgian endive, arugula, and dandelion, have been discovered by upscale restaurateurs. There is now a demand to have them available year-round. How dull. I look forward to mâche and endive in the winter. That is their season, and they are fresh and alive, while corn and beans are limp specimens on the produce shelf or boxed in the store's freezer.

Doesn't this seasonality limit the meals? Not at all. Rather than being restricting, this garden larder is liberating and inspirational. Instead of canned or frozen peas in November, you eat fresh broccoli, crisp sugarloaf chicory, or a piquant sorrel soup. Instead of stale California head lettuce, your February salad is made from fresh mâche, Belgian endive, claytonia, and arugula. Canned corn in April? No way, when your garden offers fresh ingredients for creamed spinach, parsnip tempura, or a dandelion soufflé.

In my grandfather's day, people celebrated the seasonality and variety of the home garden. They knew that one cabbage tasted best fresh in June and that another made the best sauerkraut. This was the pea for eating fresh and that the one for drying. They were familiar with 50 different apples and 20 pears. They knew when these were ripe and which blended best for cider or complemented the flavor of this or that cheese. We can recover such civilized living again.

The potential for year-round gardening reminds me of an article I once read in which wild-food gourmet Euell Gibbons led a group of novices on a food-gathering expedition in New York's Central Park. The participants were astonished by what was available. It had always been there, but they had never looked because they didn't realize the possibilities. The same is true of your home garden. There may be a lot of food there already after the summer garden ends.

For example, if you grow Swiss chard, it should be edible right up until hard winter weather, and it should rebound in spring unless you live in the far north. After you cut the main head of a broccoli plant, many smaller side shoots emerge and will keep producing throughout the fall if you harvest them. Any onions that you missed at harvest time will sprout and grow tender greens in the spring. You might want to leave the small ones in the garden on purpose. A large number of common crops will survive the winter even in the coldest climates if there is consistent snow cover (snow is a wonderful insulator). If you add cold frames and a few nontraditional crops to your garden, the four-season harvest will quickly become a reality.

The Inviting Garden

Too often the impediments to garden success are less in the garden soil than in the gardener's mind. The neglected end-of-summer garden will often inhibit your participation in harvest extension. It is what I call a "subconscious garden negative." Anyone who has gone out to a summer garden in the fall knows the depressing feeling of the end of the growing season. The look of a spent garden is hardly uplifting. Neglected, untidy, and worn-out are all conditions we avoid. Perhaps we see some of our own mortality in the "death" of summer. But nature doesn't die off in the fall; some of its plants do. In the four-season garden, fall isn't an end but a place on the continuum. New possibilities open up for those plants that thrive in new conditions.

I have been fortunate in my life to know many marvelous human beings who, even in old age, have kept themselves spiritually young. It is obvious why they are such refreshing company: they never stop participating, learning, producing, and contributing. That is exactly the spirit represented by the four-season garden. Specific seasons come and go, but the spirit perseveres throughout the year. You avoid the end-of-season feeling by cleaning up each crop as it matures and replanting that area. The four-season garden is perpetually renewed and always looks like spring and summer. Like those treasured friends, this garden is refreshing to be around, and it encourages your participation.

The Spacious Garden

Along with keeping the garden young at heart, I also suggest keeping it spacious. Like the companions we cherish, the spaces we willingly inhabit are those that welcome and comfort us. A crowded and tangled garden is as uninviting as a spent and neglected one. If the garden is not easy to enter and walk through, it will, subconsciously, keep you out. To that end, the distance between plants and rows in the garden should be less a function of the space requirements of the plants than a function of the space requirements of the gardener. Make the rows shorter and fewer or the beds narrower and the paths wider. Use succession plantings of zucchini, for example, and remove the large, sprawling plants when the new ones start to bear. Allow more comfortable space for picking, nibbling, planting, and cultivating. The highly intensive garden may be more productive spatially, but if it keeps you out, it is far less productive practically.

It is ideal to be able to pop out to the garden for that last-minute handful of basil, parsley, or chives or to pull some radishes and baby carrots for snacks when company arrives. If your spur-of-the-moment garden visit requires any sort of balancing, tiptoeing, or rope swinging to reach the desired crops, the layout is too crowded. If the visit involves struggling with an old gate that always sticks or being garroted by the clothesline, access

Fig. 1

*The back door kitchen
garden*

is a problem. Very often, only by removing the negatives do you become aware of the powerful effect they have had. Try making your garden smaller, simpler, and more open. I also encourage you to locate the garden next to the kitchen door or as close to it as possible. Then the invitation to the garden larder will be not only pleasant but also close at hand.

The Guilt-Free Garden

Another subconscious garden negative is garden guilt. With year-round production, there are no mistakes or penalties to be paid for temporary neglect. This is the "don't worry, be happy" school of gardening. There is always tomorrow. If some other important aspect of your life calls you away and weeds dominate the beans or the new planting germinates poorly, just erase the problem and start again. Take a hoe and a rake, clean off the area, and replant it with whatever crop comes next in the sequence. Sure, one crop may be missing, but there are plenty of others. I guarantee you that professionals who grow a wide range of crops will fail on a few of them every year.

This is no longer the old "I only had one chance to plant and I goofed" situation that you may dread. In the four-season garden, you have many chances and many seasons to come. Everything, even so-called failures, can have a purpose. Look on the weeds as the soil savers that they are—in essence a short-term green manure. Their roots have aerated the soil, and their tops will add to the bounty of the compost heap. Move ahead, get out the seed packets, and plant something new. This process has no penalties, only rewards; no disasters, only opportunities.

Let's dispense with another garden negative: produce envy. Do your yields measure up? Is your lettuce as big as the supermarket variety? Forget all that stuff. This is your garden, and the rules are your own. You don't need to do what the pros do, what your neighbor does, or what any book says. The commercial standards of industrial agriculture are meaningless in the home garden. Besides, they are achieved with innumerable chemicals that artificially expand and disguise poor produce by doping up the plant's metabolism. In addition to not wanting to eat such produce, I certainly don't want to emulate the techniques.

Enormous size should not be a criterion for garden success. It usually indicates overfertilization. If the vegetables look healthy and taste good, they are winners. Take lettuce as an example. If at the start you have trouble growing large heads of lettuce or prefer not to, plant 2 to 4 times as many, plant them closer together, and harvest them small. You now have baby lettuce (a gourmet item), which has taste and tenderness virtues all its own. In addition to enjoying greater variety, you will also experience far fewer pest and disease problems by harvesting your crops in their youth. Commercial standards are concerned with packing, shipping, and wholesale marketing, not flavor, tenderness, and eating pleasure. Ignore the commercial hype and concentrate on the standards that really count. Furthermore, I guarantee that if you follow the simple soil-improving suggestions in Chapter 2, your vegetables will not take a backseat to anyone's.

The Organic Garden

Let's take a moment to discuss the benefits of organic gardening. I have no fearful tales to tell. I have no moral sermon. I have no intention of drowning you in pages of factual data. I garden organically, as I have for 25 years, for very practical reasons. Organic methods are simpler and work better. That's right, they work better. Chemical agriculture is one of the great myths of the 20th century. The chemical devotees swear that chemical fertilizers and pesticides are indispensable. In my experience, they are totally superfluous. They are necessary only as a crutch for the weaknesses of industrial food production.

Basically, organic gardening means a partnership with nature. Nature's gardeners are numerous and eager to help. Millions of beneficial organisms (everything from bacteria to earthworms to ground beetles) thrive in a fertile soil, and they make things go right if the gardener encourages them. The gardener does that by understanding the natural processes of the soil and aiding them with compost. The inherent stability and resilience of natural systems can be on your side if you work with them. Organic gardening is a great adventure, an expedition into a deeper and more satisfying understanding of vegetable production. You are now a participant rather than a spectator. You share creation.

A delightful bonus of organic soil care is the quality of the vegetables. To me, food is not a commodity to be produced as cheaply as possible. It is the living matter that fuels my system. I agree with the conclusion of many other organic growers around the world that crops grown in a fertile soil are higher in food quality. It is not just the absence of the negatives—pesticides and chemicals—that makes the difference. It is also the presence of the positives. Whether the difference in composition is due to the amount of enzymes, the amino acid balance, trace minerals, unknown factors, or all of the above is yet unknown. There are many theories. There is also increasing evidence that the biological quality of plants is vitally important to human health. I am convinced that future investigations will confirm the value of food quality, just as present research has already confirmed the essential place of vegetables in the diet.

The key to vegetable quality is the quality of the soil in which the vegetables are grown. Soil is the raw material. Soil quality is influenced by the practices of the gardener. For a soil to be truly alive and productive, it must contain plenty of organic matter, plus the full spectrum of minerals. The soil can then feed the vegetables. A vital, alive soil will produce vital, alive vegetables. Very simple and successful backyard techniques for building a live soil are presented in Chapters 2 and 3.

Once a product has been grown or manufactured, the next greatest effect on its quality is how it is stored or taken care of. A carefully crafted tool made of steel and left in the rain will soon rust and deteriorate. Vegetables are no different. Freshness influences both their nutrient content and and their flavor. The nutritive value falls quickly after harvest unless vegetables are cooled and kept moist. But no matter how carefully they are preserved, vegetables that are 5 days en route from a faraway state or country to your supermarket have lost a great deal of their value.

In the pages to come, I outline a four-season harvest system for the home garden. It's what I have arrived at after years of refining and adapting ideas from around the world. I feel comfortable presenting this system because I have used these techniques long enough to guarantee that they will work. If you have no preferences of your own, this is a good place to start. But don't stop with my advice. You can do better. Always be curious enough to adjust and fine-tune. Over the years, you have put your own stamp on many other important activities you do regularly. Anything as much a part of your life as your food supply should be as personal as possible.

CHAPTER 2

THE LIVING SOIL:
COMPOST

So often, the obvious solution is right at our fingertips, but it looks so simple that we fail to notice. Generations of gardeners have consistently come up with the same chain of logic: a fertile soil is the key to growing garden vegetables; compost is the key to a fertile soil. The first step in the four-season harvest is learning to make good compost. It is not difficult to do. Compost wants to happen.

Compost is the end result of the decomposition of organic matter. It is basically a brown to black crumbly material that looks like rich chocolate fudge cake. Compost is produced by managing the breakdown of organic material in a pile called a compost heap. Compost enhances soil fertility because fertile soil and compost share a prolific population of organisms whose food is decaying organic matter. These organisms' life processes make nutrients from the organic matter and from the soil minerals available to growing plants. A fertile soil is filled with life. Compost is the life preserver.

Gardeners are not alone in their reverence for compost. Poets have found it equally inspiring. Andrew Hudgins, in a poem titled "Compost: An Ode," refers to the role of the compost heap in uniting life and death: "a leisurely collapsing of the thing into its possibilities." John Updike reminds us that since "all process is reprocessing," the forest can consume its fallen trees and "the woodchuck corpse vanish to leave behind a poem." Walt Whitman marvels at how composting allows the earth to grow "such sweet things out of such corruptions."

Good compost, like any other carefully crafted product, is not an accident. It comes about through a process involving microorganisms, organic matter, air, moisture, and time that can be orchestrated in anyone's backyard. No machinery is necessary, and no moving parts need repair. All you need to do is heap up the ingredients as specified in the next section and let nature's decomposers do the work.

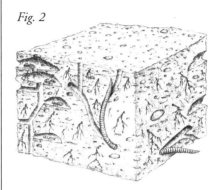

Fig. 2

The living soil

Compost Ingredients

The ingredients for the heap are the organic waste materials produced in most yards, gardens, and kitchens. The more eclectic the list of ingredients, the better the compost. That is only logical. The plant wastes that go into your compost heap were once plants that grew because they were able to incorporate the nutrients they needed. If you mix together a broad range of plants with different mineral makeups, the resulting compost will cover the nutrient spectrum.

I suggest dividing your compost ingredients into two categories based on their age and composition. I call the two categories *green* and *brown.*

The green ingredients include mostly young, moist, and fresh materials. They are the most active decomposers. Examples are kitchen wastes such as apple peels, leftovers, carrot tops, and bread and garden wastes such as grass clippings, weeds, fresh pea vines, outer cabbage leaves, and dead chipmunks. The average house and yard produce wastes such as these in surprising quantities. National solid waste data indicate that approximately 25 percent of household trash consists of food scraps and yard waste.

The brown ingredients are usually older and drier than the green ones, and they decompose more slowly. Examples are dried grass stems, old cornstalks, dried pea and bean vines, reeds, and old hay. The brown category is usually not well represented in the average backyard. To start, I suggest that you purchase straw, the best brown ingredient of all. Straw is the stem that holds up the amber waves of grain in crops such as wheat, oats, barley, and rye.

After the heads containing the grains are harvested, the straw is baled as a by-product. You can purchase straw a few bales at a time from feed stores, riding stables, or a good garden supply store.

The advantage of straw as the brown ingredient is that it will almost guarantee the success of your composting efforts. When home gardeners encounter smelly failures in their attempts to make good compost, the fault usually lies with the lack of a proper brown ingredient. In years to come, when you become an expert at composting, you may choose to expand your repertoire beyond this beginner's technique, but it is the most reliable method I know for beginners or experts.

Building the Compost Heap

Pick a site near the garden so the finished compost will be close at hand. Whenever possible, place the heap under the branches of a deciduous tree so there will be shade in hot weather and sunlight to thaw the heap in spring. A site near the kitchen makes it convenient to add kitchen scraps. Access to a hose is handy for those times when the heap needs extra moisture. If the site is uphill from the garden, the heavy work of wheelbarrowing loads of compost will have gravity on its side.

Build the compost heap by alternating layers of brown ingredients with layers of green ones. I start with a layer of straw about 3 inches deep, then add 1 to 6 inches of green ingredients, another 3 inches of straw, and then more green ingredients. The thickness of the green layer depends on the nature of the materials. Loose, open material such as green bean vines or tomato stems can be applied in a thicker (6-inch) layer, while denser material that might mat together, such as kitchen scraps or grass clippings, should be layered thinly (1 to 2 inches). These thicknesses are a place for you to start, but you will learn to modify them as conditions require.

I sprinkle a thin covering of soil on top of each green layer. Make the soil ¼ to 1 inch deep depending on what type of green material is available. If you have just added a layer of weeds with soil on their roots, you can skip the soil covering for that layer. The addition of soil to the compost heap has both a physical and a microbiological effect: physical because certain soil constitu-

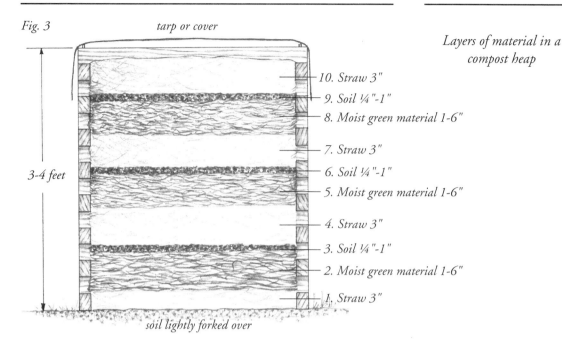

Fig. 3

tarp or cover

Layers of material in a compost heap

10. *Straw 3"*
9. *Soil ¼"-1"*
8. *Moist green material 1-6"*

7. *Straw 3"*
6. *Soil ¼"-1"*
5. *Moist green material 1-6"*

4. *Straw 3"*
3. *Soil ¼"-1"*
2. *Moist green material 1-6"*
1. *Straw 3"*

3-4 feet

soil lightly forked over

ents (clay particles and minerals) have been shown to enhance the decomposition of organic matter; microbiological because soil contains millions of microorganisms, which are needed to break down the organic material in the heap. These bacteria, fungi, and other organisms multiply in the warm, moist conditions as decomposition is initiated. If your garden is very sandy or gravelly, I suggest finding some clay to add to the heap as the soil layer. As an additional benefit, the clay will improve the balance of soil particle sizes in your garden.

Heap Dynamics

The reason for layering the ingredients is that the decomposition process is akin to a smoldering fire. If you use care in building the heap, it will "light" every time. The slow combustion of the compost heap is an exothermic reaction—that is, it gives off heat. The microorganisms create the heat by breaking down the organic material. Unlike the sticks in a camp fire, however, these combustibles should not be dry. They should be slightly moist, like a muggy day. Sir Albert Howard, an early compost enthusiast, described the ideal moisture level as akin to that of a squeezed-out sponge.

The temperature inside an active heap can reach 140° to 160°F. In this microbiologically powered furnace, the brown ingredients provide the fuel. Straw, for instance, is a carbonaceous material with a high ratio of carbon to nitrogen. The green ingredients provide the fire. They are nitrogenous materials containing a higher ratio of nitrogen. All the millions of organisms in the heap use the nitrogen to help break down the carbon structure of organic material into a humuslike end product. The combination of green and brown materials provides the ideal balance between carbon and nitrogen for optimal breakdown.

As with any other fire, there is one more crucial requirement for the compost heap—air. The beneficial bacteria that create the heat, decomposition, and ultimate conversion of the ingredients into compost are aerobic (that is, requiring air). This explains why straw is perfect for successful composting. Straw stems, besides providing the carbonaceous fuel for this bacterial fire, also ensure aeration. They are hollow, like drinking straws, and tend to lie across each other loosely. That structure allows air to enter easily, in contrast to a heap composed only of green material, which can mat together. When there is plenty of air, the aerobic bacteria can breathe deeply and multiply. When they are active in great numbers, decomposition proceeds smoothly and without odor. If composting fails, it is usually because the ingredients are packed into an airless mass and the activities of the aerobic bacteria are inhibited.

When the conditions for composting are less than optimum, the reaction of the heap will help you determine the problem. There are two common symptoms. The first is odor. A well-made compost heap is odorless. A bad smell indicates that something is amiss. When the heap is too wet or compacted the process becomes anaerobic (without air), and a different bacterial population takes over. The anerobic bacteria create sewage-type odors. If the heap is made with too much fire (green nitrogenous material) and not enough fuel (brown carbonaceous material), it will have a strong ammonia odor because the bacteria are volatilizing the extra nitrogen. You can improve both situations by forking the material into a new pile alongside and piling it more loosely with additional layers of straw.

The second symptom is failure to heat up. If the heap is too dry, the bacteria are inhibited, as they thrive best under moist

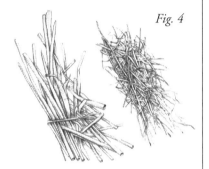

Fig. 4

Hollow straw stems allow more air into the heap than does hay.

conditions. Normally the combination of ingredients will be adequately moist. But when the weather has been dry, you may want to add water. That is most easily accomplished with a watering can or hose sprayer. Add enough water to each layer as you build to ensure that it is moist. Remember the analogy of the squeezed-out sponge. Another reason the heap may fail to heat up is an excess of fuel (carbon) and not enough fire (nitrogen). In that case, you can try to stimulate the bacteria with an organic, high-nitrogen liquid fertilizer such as fish emulsion. Dissolve half a cup into a watering can, make holes in the heap with a crowbar or pointed stake, and pour in the solution. In a pinch, you can use molasses (same proportions), sour milk diluted with equal parts of water, or any other bacterial food. This should initiate the composting process by getting hoards of bacteria off to a running start.

I mention these problems in case they arise. But if you follow my heap-building directions, your composting should run smoothly. When fire, fuel, moisture, and air are in balance, the heap will purr like a contented kitten.

Compost Bins

When making compost, it helps to enclose it in a container. A number of backyard compost containers are available. I have found 2 models that I like best. First are the ventilated bins made from recycled plastic, such as the *Biostack* (see appendix). These are about 36 inches square. They are nice if you plan to make daily additions of kitchen scraps because the ingredients are protected from 4-legged raiders by strong sides and a lid. Plan on having 2 bins so that one can supply usable compost while you are filling the other. The other model is made of wooden slats sawed from waste wood. The slats are put together like a Lincoln Log kit. They are held together at the corners with metal rods that fit into predrilled holes. Wooden-slat bins are about 3 to 3 ½ feet square. If you want a larger heap for serious quantities of compost, buy 2 wooden-slat kits and make a hexagonal or octagonal structure with 6 or 8 sides.

You can also make a heap by using bales of straw as walls. That way, you get double duty from the straw—first as a container and then as an ingredient. Lay the bales around an

Fig. 5

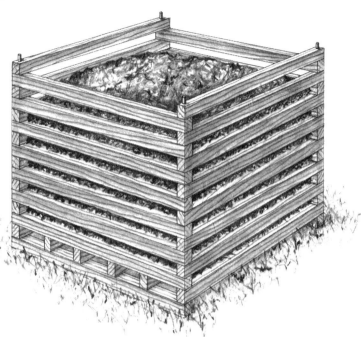

*A wooden compost container,
assembled from a kit.*

open center as if you were building a playhouse with large straw bricks. Leave small spaces between the bales for air to enter (see Fig. 5). I make the inside dimensions anywhere from 4 to 6 feet square. A heap smaller than 3 feet square won't have enough volume to hold heat and will decompose slowly. A heap larger than 8 feet square is too large for air to reach the center. Even with a 6-foot-square heap, I put a stake in the center while building the layers to allow direct air access to the middle of the heap. I then remove the stake when the heap has finished decomposing.

As I fill the heap I build the walls progressively to a height of 2 bales stacked cut end down. A heap with inside dimensions of 5 to 6 feet square requires 16 to 20 bales of straw. After a year or two, when the bales begin to break down and no longer hold together as walls, they become ingredients in a subsequent heap. Bales tied with wire or plastic will last longer than those tied with baling twine. The straw becomes moist and partially decomposed while it serves as walls. That prepares it perfectly for its next role as compost ingredient.

Another advantage of straw walls is that the contents of the heap stay moist and warm right to the edge. As a result, the initial decomposition is often so complete that the heap may not need

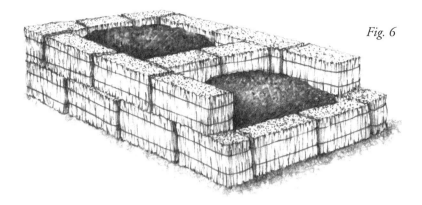

Fig. 6

A straw bale compost container

to be turned (see page 24). The bales also provide insulation in cooler weather, which is useful for a heap made in late summer. The heating process can keep going longer into the fall. Both the store-bought bins and the straw bales will give you a heap that looks very neat, contains the ingredients successfully, and lets in plenty of air.

Ideally, you should build the heap over the course of a couple of months, but that schedule is very flexible. It is best if 6 or more layers can go on initially. Then there is enough mass for the heating to begin. Every few days afterward, you can add another couple of layers. The initial heating is stimulated by the continuous addition of new fuel, and the heat moves up layer by layer. The heap may seem to build quickly, but as the breakdown progresses, the material will settle. When you have reached 3 to 4 feet and the material is no longer settling, add a final layer of straw to complete the heap. Active breakdown will continue until the heat begins to decline.

A cover over the heap is a valuable addition at this point. The cover prevents excessive moisture from getting in during wet periods and keeps the heap from drying out during times of drought. Plastic bins include their own fitted covers. For wooden-slat bins or straw-bale heaps, I use a tarp with a weight hanging from each corner so it won't blow off. If you think that the heap needs more moisture, remove the cover on rainy days. During winter, a wooden lid over my straw-bale heap keeps the snow out, yet is easily lifted for adding kitchen scraps and layers of straw.

The heat of composting reaches its peak a few weeks after the heap is completed and then dies down. By then the microorganisms have used up the easy fuel of the initial breakdown process.

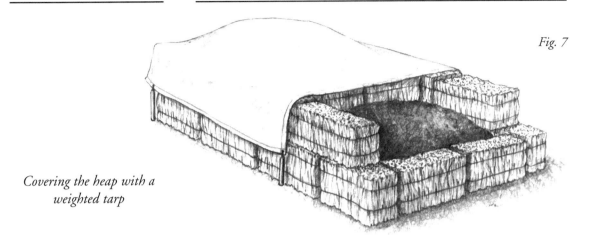

Fig. 7

Covering the heap with a weighted tarp

The gardener can speed up the subsequent breakdown by turning the heap. This remixing is akin to stirring a fire or using a bellows. By increasing the aeration, you get the combustion going again. The easiest system for turning compost is to erect another heap alongside the first. Then, using a manure fork, turn the compost by forking the initial pile into the second container. I try to shake each forkful as I dump it into the new space so as to loosen the material and allow more air to enter. If the outer edges of the heap are less decomposed than the center, try to place them in the middle of the new heap. Once the pile has been turned, cover it and start building again on the original site.

Autumn Leaves and Animal Manure

I specifically haven't mentioned autumn leaves, wood chips, or sawdust. They are in the brown category, but I don't use them in my compost heaps. Wood chips and sawdust take so long to decompose that I have never been happy with the resulting compost. Autumn leaves are a wonderful soil improver, but I don't include them because they mat together and can create airless conditions in a compost heap. Leaf decomposition takes place primarily through the action of fungi rather than bacteria. Thus, it seems to work better if leaves are piled separately. If a few leaves blow into your compost heap, they don't present a problem, but in quantity they are best used to make leaf mold.

Leaf mold is the horticultural term for decomposed autumn leaves. You make it by putting leaves in a pile and waiting 2 to

3 years. A circular container 4 to 6 feet in diameter made of snow fence or stiff wire mesh holds leaves effectively. If the leaves are dry, wet them with a hose as you pile them. You can also stomp on them inside the bin to make room for more. Compaction doesn't hinder the fungal decomposition of wet leaves. Leaf mold has traditionally been used like compost as a general soil enhancer. I prefer to use it mainly for crops in the cabbage (Cruciferae) and carrot (Umbelliferae) families. It works like a health tonic for those crops. Leaves also can be a very effective soil enhancer if they are tilled directly into the garden in the fall.

Animal manure has been a favorite soil amendment for generations of horticulturists. Even before the horse and buggy was replaced by the automobile, however, gardeners who had no animals were looking for additional sources of organic soil amendments. Some of the early books on making compost from vegetable matter called compost "artificial manure." These early investigators learned that by composting mixed plant wastes, they got a product that worked better than the traditional rotted animal manures because the ingredients were more varied and the moisture and aeration levels during the breakdown period could be managed more precisely.

If you have access to animal manures, by all means use them. Add them to the soil only when they are well rotted, not fresh. The nitrogen in fresh manure can be caustic to plant material. The soil-enhancing value of manure is especially good if the animals were bedded on straw rather than sawdust or shavings. The best animal manures are horse, cow, sheep, and goat. Rather than putting manure directly on the garden, add it as another ingredient in the compost heap. I try to limit the quantity to no more than 10 percent of the total. You can put a layer of manure on top of the brown or green layer as you build the heap. Be careful with poultry manure. It is very concentrated, and the nutrients are imbalanced. I have always thought poultry manure caused more problems than it solved.

How Do You Know When It's Ready?

Compost has a number of stages of readiness, each one better than the one before. If the heap heats up properly, the compost is usable after the heap cools down. At this stage, you can still distinguish some of the original materials. Although not yet fully broken down, this is good compost. Further breakdown will take place in the soil after application. It is best to mix this rough compost into the soil at the end of the outdoor season so the decomposition can continue over the winter. You can use it as a top dressing at other times of the year. If you want finer compost immediately, you can sift this first stage compost through a wire mesh screen.

If you want all the compost to be dark, crumbly, and more thoroughly decomposed, you will need to turn the heap to initiate the second flush of heating and decomposition. This second stage of compost is a better product. Almost none of the original materials can be distinguished. Most of the compost is crumbly, very dark, and sweet smelling. This compost can be used almost anywhere.

The finest compost, like good wine or cheese, is a product of time. It needs to mature. To achieve full compost maturity, you must turn the heap a second time, cover it, and let the compost age until it is 1 to 2 years old. At that point, it will achieve a wonderful chocolate fudge cake texture throughout. A 1- to 2-year-old, well-decomposed vegetable compost is the definition of soil fertility. It comes as close as you can get to a miracle plant food. This is the quality of compost I prefer for all indoor and outdoor garden use. It is the secret to the success of the homemade potting soil mixtures described in Chapter 5.

A specialist on composting would describe this mature compost as "well humified." Humus is the end stage of decomposition. It is the longest lasting, most effective soil organic matter. Humus in the soil provides stable and balanced conditions for plant nutrition and root growth. A well-humified compost has amazing powers for enhancing plant growth and suppressing diseases.

The surest way to have plenty of mature compost available is to get started now, whatever the season. While you are waiting for the first heap to mature, keep making new heaps so you will always have more coming along. Then when the first heap is ready, you won't be stingy. Compost is such a wonderful medium for growing plants that once you start using it in the vegetable garden, you will want more for the flowers, shrubs, and bare spots in the lawn. To produce more compost, you will need more raw materials. Extra compost materials can be acquired in a number of ways, outlined in the next section.

Finding More Ingredients

An unused area of your lawn can be turned into a very attractive source of green matter for the compost heap by planting it to alfalfa. Alfalfa is a favorite forage with livestock farmers because it grows vigorously; has deep drought-resistant roots; and will regrow 12 to 16 inches tall after each cutting, allowing at least 4 cuts per season. Alfalfa will grow successfully in any sunny, well-drained site as long as the soil is not acidic. Alfalfa likes a pH of 7. (You can correct soil acidity by adding limestone.) Alfalfa is easy to establish. Just scatter the seeds on bare ground, rake them in, and keep the soil moist until germination. Planting alfalfa is no different from planting a lawn. Seeds for an alfalfa variety suited to your area can be purchased from your local farm supply store.

I mow my backyard alfalfa with an old-fashioned scythe. Mowing with a scythe is pleasurable exercise and a wonderful skill to learn. If you take it up, I predict that the scythe will become one of your favorite yard tools and you will prefer it to a power mower or weed wacker for cleaning up those odd rough areas. I use a European-style scythe (see appendix). The key to success with a scythe, once the basic motion has been mastered, is to keep the blade sharp. As with any edge tool, the difference between sharp and dull is the difference between pleasure and drudgery.

I mow the alfalfa as I need it for the green layers in the heap. The best management practice is to mow the area every time the first blossoms appear. The patch is more productive that way, and the regrowth will be even. Alfalfa has deep roots and is a strong feeder on nutrients from the lower levels of the soil. It is very high in minerals and is a valuable addition to any garden fertility-improvement scheme. Before planting, I fertilize the patch with the rock minerals described later in this chapter. In good soil, an alfalfa planting can be productive for 10 years or more. When the alfalfa thins out and other plants invade and lower the productivity of the patch, you should till the soil and replant.

You will become aware of many other sources of organic matter as soon as you become interested in composting. A time-honored source of compost materials is your neighbors' yards. "Hi, George, I'd love to have that pile of (trimmings, leaves, rotten apples) if you have no use for it." I know enthusiasts who extend that search beyond immediate neighbors to the local area by carrying an empty trash container in the back of their car. The container is usually full of weeds, spoiled vegetables, or grass clippings when they arrive home. Weeds are a particularly valuable addition to compost, since they are vigorous, heavy-feeding plants with a high mineral content. It is best to collect weeds before they go to seed. If you see a particularly lush area of weeds, ask if you can cut them. Most people are delighted to oblige. You may acquire a reputation as an eccentric, but you can console yourself with the knowledge that you are setting a good example. Recycling is important. Nature is the classic recycler. If we use nature as a model, we won't lack for direction.

Using Compost

Once you have a quantity of dark, crumbly compost, what do you do with it? Rather than fork it in deeply, I spread it on top of the soil and just mix it in shallowly. I find the quality of plant growth is superior if I duplicate nature's system of leaving organic matter on the surface to be mixed in by earthworms and other soil creatures. I help out by mixing the compost into the top 2 inches of soil with a curved-tine cultivator (see appendix). The one I prefer is about 7 inches wide and has 3 large tines with the center tine offset from the others. I work the tool back and forth gently and shallowly like a lightweight, hand-powered tiller. It incorporates the compost without damaging the soil structure.

How much compost should you spread? Let's see if we can calculate an answer in a way that makes sense. One cubic foot of compost will logically cover a 12-square-foot area to a depth of 1 inch. If, for example, your garden dimensions are 900 square feet (30 by 30 feet), you would need 75 cubic feet of compost (900 square feet divided by 12 square feet) for a 1-inch-deep

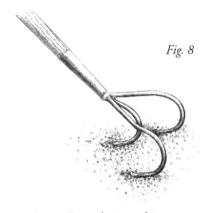

Fig. 8

Curved-tine cultivator

application over the whole garden. A compost heap 5 feet long by 5 feet wide by 3 feet tall would contain 75 cubic feet of compost.

Do you need to apply compost to a depth of 1 inch? By old-time vegetable-growing standards, 1 inch of compost averages out to about 75 tons to the acre. Thus, a 1-inch layer of finished compost can be considered a very generous rate of use. I recommend being generous at the start, even if that means purchasing rotted manure or peat moss. Peat moss alone is an inadequate soil enhancer but used in a half-and-half mixture with compost, it will serve you quite well. Once you have enough compost, a maintenance application of ¼ to ½ inch per year should be more than enough to maintain and improve your garden's productivity.

How do you figure out the depth of compost you are spreading without using a measuring stick and wasting a lot of time? Let's say you have a garden bed 30 inches wide by 15 feet long. The surface area of that plot is 37½ square feet, or 5,400 square inches. To put a 1-inch layer of compost on a 5,400-square-inch area would require 5,400 cubic inches of compost; a ½-inch layer would require half that. A 5-gallon pail holds about 1,150 cubic inches. Thus, spreading 2½ 5-gallon pails of compost would give you 2,875 cubic inches, or a close approximation of ½ inch of compost on an area 30 inches wide by 15 feet long. Computations like these may seem complicated, but once you have the figures, they make your gardening more efficient and the results more predictable.

Mineral Amendments

As I have said, a good compost will usually provide all the nutrients necessary for a productive garden. I do, however, suggest adding 3 mineral supplements. The most familiar of these is limestone, which is added to the soil to counteract acidity. You may not be familiar with the other 2 supplements—phosphate rock and greensand. They are ground-up rock products that contain a broad spectrum of plant nutrients. You add them to the soil to make sure all the minerals necessary for healthy plant growth are available—a soil fertility insurance policy, if you will.

Limestone, or lime, is finely ground limestone rock, which contains mostly calcium carbonate. Lime is applied to acidic soils to raise the pH. pH is a measure of soil acidity on a scale of 1 to 14. The lower the number, the greater the acidity: 7 is neutral, above 7 is alkaline, and below 7 is acidic. Most of the natural processes in the soil that affect the growth of garden vegetables function optimally at a pH of 6 to 7 (slightly acidic). You can determine your soil's pH by purchasing a testing kit from a garden supply catalog or by having it tested professionally. The local extension service can help you find out where to get that done. If the soil is too acidic (below 6), add limestone by sprinkling it on the soil and mixing it in. Your soil test recommendations will suggest how much limestone to use. If the soil is too alkaline (above 7), adding extra organic matter such as an acidic peat moss is an effective solution.

Phosphate rock and colloidal phosphate are slow-release sources of phosphorus. They are mined from rock and clay deposits containing 20 to 30 percent phosphates. If phosphate rock is unavailable, bone meal is another slow-release source of phosphorus. Adding phosphate rock or bone meal is a good policy because phosphorus is the nutrient most likely to be deficient in your garden soil. When you start your garden, add phosphate rock to the soil at a rate of 10 pounds per 100 square feet.

Greensand is a mineral mined from old sea-bottom deposits. It is a slow-release source of potassium and trace elements. Potassium is an important nutrient for plant health and vigor. Trace elements such as zinc, copper, molybdenum, boron, and manganese, though required in very small quantities, are vital for plant and animal well-being. In most cases, if you add a compost of mixed ingredients to the soil, it should have no lack of potassium or trace elements. But just to make sure, I add greensand. I recommend 10 pounds per 100 square feet the first year.

The mineral nutrients in these powdered rock products are not highly water soluble, unlike the treated ingredients in chemical fertilizers. They don't need to be, as the activities of microorganisms, which are nourished by organic matter in the soil, will make these nutrients available to plants at a balanced rate.

Initially, I apply phosphate rock and greensand directly on the garden soil. After that, I find it easier and more effective to sprinkle these products very lightly on the green layer of the compost heap. For my 30-by-60-foot garden, I add 20 pounds of each mineral to my compost each year. That is more than enough to make up for the minerals removed from the soil in the form of harvested crops. A number of scientific trials have determined that adding rock powders to the compost heap enhances their availability for plant use, since the soluble acids in humus formation begin to dissolve the rock nutrients.

In addition to the minerals mentioned, you may find one of the commercially available seaweed products useful. Seaweed is sold in a dried form to be added directly to the soil or in various liquid extractions for spraying on the leaves of plants as a pick-me-up. Although it can be expensive, dried seaweed offers great benefits for some soils. If the soil fertility seems slow getting off the mark, seaweed is an option you may want to explore. The liquid extractions are used as natural plant stimulants. Their action has been described as "rescue nutrition" for below-par plants. They can be useful as palliatives in the soil-building years but shouldn't be needed once soil fertility is established.

The natural processes that you nurture by adding compost and rock minerals to your garden soil are the same processes that have been making soil nutrients available to plants for millions of years. If you wish to read a more detailed discussion of the subject, you can consult my book for small farmers, *The New Organic Grower* (Chelsea Green, 1989).

CHAPTER 3

The Outdoor Garden:
Planning
and Preparing

C risp *French Breakfast* radishes with the dew still on them; baby beets—sweet, tender, and harvested just before dinner; tiny, crunchy carrots that taste like candy; the delightful aroma of herbs growing outside the kitchen door. With rewards like these awaiting the palate, nothing defeats the determined gardener. From the celebrated Aran Islanders layering seaweed and sand together to make soil on barren rock to the deepest city dweller with pots of treasured vegetables on the windowsill, the urge to grow edibles is unstoppable.

The amount of work involved in creating a garden depends to some extent on where you live. If you are blessed with the perfect location and ideal soil, such as the deep, rich earth of the Midwest, you will have less to do when starting out. If your site was not blessed by Mother Nature, you will need to expend some effort making conditions hospitable for garden plants. But it's not a major project. You just have to supplement and modify what nature gave you.

Preparing the Garden Site

When I began gardening on my place in Maine, the soil test showed a pH of 4.3 (very acidic), and a note from the soil scientist warned that the ground did not seem suitable for agriculture. Well, every soil can be made suitable. I began by spreading limestone to make the soil less acidic. That got suitability for agriculture off to a running start. The soil was very sandy, so I added some clay from the house foundation and tilled it in thoroughly. (If the soil had been too clayey, I would have tilled in a lot of peat moss. Because of the quantities involved, adding sand to a clay soil doesn't work as well as adding clay to a sandy soil.) My soil had too many stones, so I removed them over time. The soil was low in minerals, so I added phosphate rock and greensand. Like most gardens, the soil needed organic matter to make the biological processes work better. I was in farm country, so I added rotted manure for the first couple of years until my composting system was on track. If no manure had been available, I would have started by tilling in an inch or more of peat moss plus some organic fertilizer mix applied at the rate recommended on the bag. Once my own compost was available, it supplied all I needed.

I also raked up autumn leaves and tilled them into parts of the garden. In the early years of establishing a garden, a rotary tiller can be a valuable aid in speeding up the transition to soil fertility. The action of the tiller tines is very effective at mixing organic or mineral supplements throughout the topsoil. If you overdo it and till frequently just to make the soil look nice, the tiller can destroy the soil structure. But when used to add organic matter and disperse minerals, a tiller is a useful tool to deepen topsoil, encourage microbiological activity, and build the foundation for long-lasting soil fertility.

It took a few years and some energy to convert that poor Maine soil into a bounteous vegetable garden, but success was inevitable. No matter what you start with, it is possible to build soil conditions for optimal plant growth. I enjoyed every minute of it. As a consequence of that effort, I learned a lot about the soil fertility principles described in this book.

Garden Microclimate

In addition to a fertile soil, you should aspire to a few other ideal conditions for your crops. The aim is to create a beneficial microclimate. *Microclimate* is the term used to define the specific climatic conditions in a small area. For example, gardens need sunlight. You may have to cut down trees to let the sun in. That doesn't mean clear-cutting your property, but you may have to choose between a tree and a garden. In some situations, trees may need to be planted. Whereas air movement in a garden is beneficial, too much wind is a problem. A windbreak will help. I planted shrubs on the north and west sides of my garden because the prevailing winds in my area are from the north and west. You also could plant a bed of raspberries or an orchard of dwarf fruit trees as a windbreak. They would then do double duty by providing food and protection from the wind.

In the same way that sunlight and windbreaks benefit the microclimate, so does the lay of the land. In northern areas, I recommend locating the garden on a south-, southeast-, or southwest-facing slope where it will warm up more quickly and stay warm longer than will a garden on a north slope. As a further refinement, select a site halfway up a slope from which the cold

Airflow around a garden site   *Fig. 9*

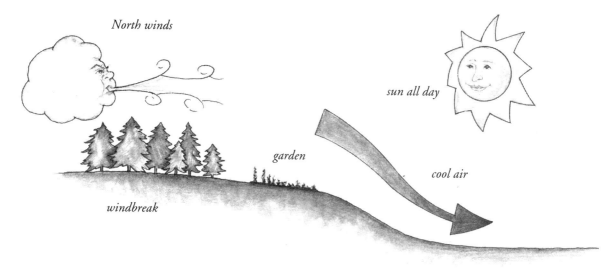

air can drain away on spring or fall nights. Cold air is heavier than warm air and actually flows downhill like water. Sites at the bottom of a slope where the cold air settles are likely to be frosty. Gardens with good air drainage usually survive a few weeks longer into the frost season.

In addition to air draining like water, you have to consider water drainage. If the soil is too wet, you may need a surface drain or, in more difficult conditions, subsurface drainage to remove excess water. Consult the local soil conservation service for technical assistance. If drainage is out of the question, you can raise the growing areas above the wetness by building sides for your beds. Use planks or concrete blocks for the sides, then fill the bed with soil up to the top.

Many gardens will benefit from some of these modifications, and a few may need all of them. But there is one overriding consideration for the four-season garden: if you are going to participate daily in your garden, it helps to have it close at hand—just like the cupboards and the refrigerator. Ideally, it should be right outside the kitchen door or as close as you can manage. It is worth sacrificing some other feature (except sunshine) for the benefits of proximity. If a back door site is not possible for the whole garden, try to have a small plot for crops such as lettuce, parsley, and chives. Your garden site should be based on the needs of both growing and eating. The better the location, the better both needs will be met.

Planning the Home Garden

Nature programs on television often feature indigenous food gatherers from remote parts of the world who successfully use the jungle or desert as their supermarket. Whatever the season, they instinctively know where to look and what to choose for the ingredients of their diet. Ideally, your home garden can be a similar food jungle—not necessarily in the sense of wild and unrestrained (although if you prefer to garden that way, go for it) but in the sense of a dependable, year-round, sustainable larder waiting to be brought to the table.

Many possible garden layouts can give you access to that larder. The easiest ones are usually the best. Organizing and maintaining your garden should be simple, pleasant work. The process of growing and harvesting the food should be just as joyful as the process of preparing and eating it so that you will look forward to both.

I like to have 2 distinct areas in the garden: space in which to walk and space in which to grow. A direct benefit from this arrangement is improved plant growth. When you walk on garden soil, you exert a pressure of around 6 to 10 pounds per square inch. That pressure closes the soil pores and seriously inhibits root expansion. Compacted soil contains less air. As with the compost heap, air is an important ingredient for optimal soil health, root growth, and microorganism activity. Roots are the invisible yet vital foundation for the aboveground parts. When root growth is below par, the whole plant suffers. I suggest that you confine your foot traffic to paths between the growing areas.

My present garden dimensions can serve as an example. Overall, my garden is 60 feet wide east to west and approximately 30 feet wide north to south. The walking spaces are 12 inches wide and the growing spaces (beds) 30 inches wide. A ground-level view of the growing garden looks like this:

Fig. 10

Ground-level view of the garden.

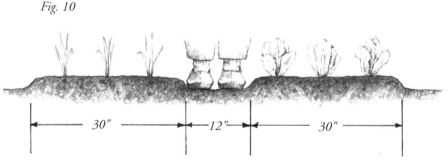

The 30-inch-wide growing spaces in my home garden are narrower than the 48-inch width used for commercial production. The wide commercial beds are keyed to tractor-based tillage, planting, cultivating, and harvesting equipment. For the home gardener, a 30-inch-wide bed is more sensible. It is easier to step over (from path to path), to straddle if you need to work above it, and to reach across when planting or harvesting.

In my garden, the beds are 15 feet long because that size fits neatly in the 60-foot dimension. They run east to west for best sun access (see Fig. 11).

The 30-inch width allows ideal spacing for most vegetable crops. If you run single rows down the middle of the bed, you can plant hills of corn, double rows of trellised peas, trellised cucumbers and tomatoes, the brassica crops, potatoes, zucchini, and so forth. Large storage beets, celery, celeriac, parsnips, and other crops of similar size have adequate space when planted at 2 rows to the bed. Lettuce, storage carrots, strawberries, and onions are among the crops that grow well at 3 rows to the bed. You will find specific spacing directions for each crop in Chapter 9.

I run many short rows across the bed for frequently sown crops or for seedlings I will later transplant. These cross rows are an easy way to maintain year-round succession plantings. It takes almost no time at all, say once a week, to sow a few short rows of radishes, mesclun mix, carrots, beet greens, arugula, spinach, or lettuce wherever there is an empty spot (see Table 1).

Bird's-eye view of garden

Fig. 11

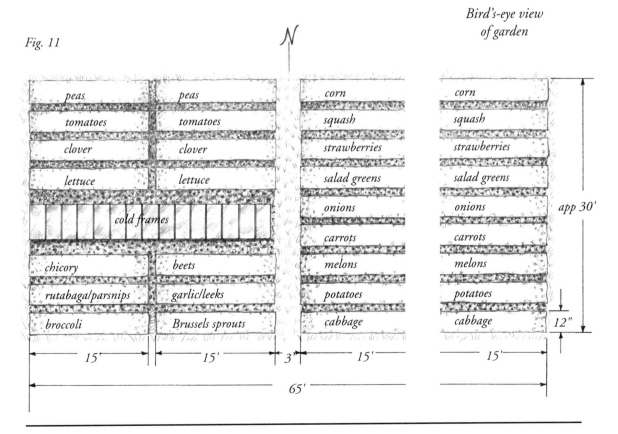

N

peas	peas	corn	corn
tomatoes	tomatoes	squash	squash
clover	clover	strawberries	strawberries
lettuce	lettuce	salad greens	salad greens
cold frames		onions	onions
		carrots	carrots
chicory	beets	melons	melons
rutabaga/parsnips	garlic/leeks	potatoes	potatoes
broccoli	Brussels sprouts	cabbage	cabbage

15'   15'   3"   15'   15'

app 30'

12"

65'

I offer my garden layout as a point of departure for those with no preferences of their own. The dimensions, shape, and scale of this layout are those that I know from experience to be comfortable and efficient. If you feel more comfortable working with ovals, triangles, squares, circles, pentagons, or spirals, use those shapes in your garden layout. The idea is for you to create a garden in which you will want to spend time.

I will make one strong suggestion with respect to layout. Your cropping area, whatever its shape, should be easily divisible. I want to encourage the small succession plantings that characterize a four-season garden. They are the best way to maintain a continual supply of vegetables. Thus, in the space where you have recently harvested some lettuce, you can remove any roots

TABLE 1

SUCCESSION PLANTING

I succession-plant many outdoor crops for a continuous harvest during the growing season. I cease sowing based on the latest dates for my area (see Table 5). Even if you think your area is too hot or too cold for these suggestions, give them a try. Experiment with heat- and cold-resistant varieties. You may be pleasantly surprised by the results.

Beans—Every 2 weeks
Beets—Every 2 weeks
Carrots—Every 2 weeks
Celery—Twice: early spring and 3 months before fall frost.
Corn—I usually sow a number of varieties with different maturity dates rather than sowing succession plantings.
Cucumbers—A second and third planting at monthly intervals will keep fruit quality high.
Lettuce and salad greens—These are the most important crops for succession plantings. I sow short rows of lettuce, chicory, arugula, mizuna, and claytonia every week or two during the growing season.
Peas—Twice: Early spring and midsummer.
Radishes—Sow every week and harvest promptly for the crispest roots.
Spinach—Sow short rows every week during spring and late summer.
Summer squash—See remarks under Cucumbers above.

and weeds, mix in a little compost, and plant 3 or 4 short rows of carrots. If you have no need for another vegetable planting, you can sow small areas of a legume such as clover to protect the soil and improve its fertility. See "Green Manures" later in this chapter for more information.

Garden Soil Structure

Figures 10 and 11 show a garden without the raised beds with which you may be familiar. I have not spent hours with the spade and fork laboriously trenching and fluffing the earth. What you see instead of raised beds could best be called sunken paths. As I said earlier, the soil is compacted only where I walk and remains loose and friable elsewhere.

You may be wondering whether it's necessary to turn and fluff the soil to keep it loose and friable. Isn't that what raised beds do? Well, that's what they try to do, but the techniques don't succeed as well as advertised. In fact, soil compaction studies have shown that disturbing the natural soil structure by fluffing and turning the soil with spade and fork is not beneficial. Undisturbed, the natural crumb structure that characterizes the work of microorganisms, earthworms, and other soil inhabitants actually has more air spaces than disturbed soil. Applying compost to the surface of the soil aids the natural process. The surface organic matter is slowly incorporated into the topsoil by the actions of earthworms and their coworkers. Further decomposition of organic matter by fungal and bacterial action goes on continuously underground. All these processes create and maintain a soil that allows air and moisture to enter, roots to grow and find nourishment, and an atmosphere which favors the life processes of all the soil inhabitants, roots included.

The subsoil is less aerated and less fertile than the topsoil but serves as a continuous source of raw materials for soil building. When the subsoil has been brought to the surface, as on a building site or other disturbed location, the best soil-building technique if you want a garden there is to add organic matter to the surface and encourage the natural processes. I have high respect for nature's system of soil layers and prefer to leave them as they are. In fact, not only do I like the topsoil on top and the subsoil below, but I also prefer not to mix them within themselves. I have found success by following the design and intention of nature's processes.

I haven't always acted this wisely. In springs long past, I dug and spaded with a vengeance. I felt so pure doing it, as if the hard work somehow ennobled me. Then one day while I was digging an area that had been undisturbed for a few years, I looked at the soil and marveled at the beautiful crumb structure that had resulted from the decomposition of organic matter by microorganisms and the equally beautiful interlacing worm tunnels—nature's underground handiwork. "Wow, what a lovely soil structure!" I exclaimed. Then I asked myself, "Why am I destroying this?"—a question I couldn't answer. So I gave up digging and began spreading compost on the surface and mixing it in shallowly (an inch or two). Right away, crop yields and quality improved. I had learned a valuable lesson: when I disturb the soil, it should be to correct my faults, not to correct nature.

Soil Aeration

In my vegetable garden, I grow mostly short-season annuals rather than perennials. By so doing, I miss a key factor in natural soil structure and aeration: the roots of perennial plants. The root systems of perennial herbs, grasses, shrubs, and trees in a truly undisturbed soil are more fibrous and permanent than the roots of annuals in a garden. Although I may have managed to add extra organic matter with compost, the soil still lacks the extra aeration provided by the perennial roots. I want to get that extra aeration without breaking up the soil structure. It would be nice if I could just lift up the soil without turning it over and allow air underneath. Fortunately, there is a wonderful tool designed to do just that.

Once a year, I aerate the soil with a broadfork. This is a 24-inch-wide, 5-tined fork with 2 handles (see Fig. 12). It is used to lift and aerate the soil without mixing the layers. The gardener holds a handle in each hand, presses the tool into the soil by stepping on the crossbar, pulls back on the handles to gently lift the soil, pulls out the tool, moves it 6 to 8 inches back, and repeats the process. You can do the same thing with a standard garden fork in smaller bites, but the broadfork is more fun. Like any classic hand tool designed for a specific job, it is a pleasure to use. With its 2 handles and wide crossbar, the motion is effortless. Helpers in my garden, especially kids, always enjoy using the broadfork, first because it is a simple tool and makes them feel athletic and coordinated, and second because of the sense of accomplishment it gives. People instinctively feel that the tool makes sense.

A gardener with a broadfork is doing by hand what large-scale organic farmers do with a winged chisel plow. I have visited organic vegetable farms in many parts of the world, and one belief most of them hold in common is the value of gentle soil lifting from below without turning. They regard it as a key practice for enhancing long-term soil productivity.

Fig. 12

Using the broadfork

Crop Rotation

In my four-season garden, as shown in Figure 11, I have 32 beds (each 30 inches by 15 feet) and 6 cold frames (each 4 by 8 feet). The garden is divided in half north and south by the cold frames and east and west by a central grassy path. I try to plant taller or trellised crops in the northern half and lower-growing crops to the south. That way the taller crops won't shade the shorter ones. An advantage of dividing the garden into a number of growing areas is that it simplifies a valuable age-old garden practice: crop rotation. That means not growing the same crop in the same spot year after year. With 32 beds, I have many options for change.

Most annual crops do best if they grow where something else grew the year before. Ideally, that something else should be an unrelated crop. For example, potatoes and tomatoes are related (both in the Solanaceae family), so one should not follow the other. But potatoes can grow where sweet corn (unrelated) grew last year, or tomatoes can follow zucchini (also unrelated). Crop rotation avoids exhausting the soil, since different crops remove different nutrients. It also avoids the buildup of pests and diseases that occurs when one crop is grown year after year in the same place.

In the year-round garden, where some beds will be planted with more than one crop per year, it is worth applying the principles of crop rotation not only as crops change year to year

TABLE 2

CROP FAMILIES

Amaryillidaceae	*Compositae*	*Polygonaceae*
Garlic	Artichoke	Sorrel
Leek	Chicory	
Onion	Dandelion	*Portulacaceae*
	Endive	Claytonia
Cruciferae	Escarole	Purslane
Arugula	Lettuce	
Broccoli	Radicchio	*Solanaceae*
Brussels sprouts		Eggplant
Cabbage	*Cucurbitaceae*	Pepper
Cabbage, Chinese	Cucumber	Potato
Cress	Melon	Tomato
Kale	Pumpkin	
Kohlrabi	Squash, summer	*Tetragoniaceae*
Mizuna	Squash, winter	New Zealand spinach
Mustard		
Radish	*Gramineae*	*Umbelliferae*
Rutabaga	Corn	Carrot
		Celery
Chenopodiaceae	*Leguminosae*	Celeriac
Beet	Bean	Parsley
Orach	Pea	Parsley root
Spinach		Parsnip
Swiss chard	*Liliaceae*	
	Asparagus	

but also within the same year. This need not be complicated. It means that if you harvest a bed of early lettuce, you should follow it with beans, carrots, or corn rather than more lettuce. The next lettuce plantings could go where early beet greens were harvested. A 3-year hiatus before a crop returns to the original spot is better than a 2-year hiatus, 4 years are better than 3. A general view of the trellised beds in my garden will serve as an example of a 4-year rotation. The representative crops are peas (which could be pole beans), tomatoes (or peppers and eggplant), squashes (including winter squashes, cucumbers, and melons), and corn (which is not trellised but is tall, so it fits in this section). Over a 4-year span, those 4 crops would rotate among the trellised beds as illustrated in Table 3.

A map of your garden plots is a useful aid. Of all the tried-and-true garden management practices, crop rotation is one of the most beneficial and economical. It costs nothing more than a little planning and imagination. There are few absolutes; it's variety that counts. So think variety when you move crops around. If you would like to read a more detailed explanation of crop rotation, consult *The New Organic Grower.*

TABLE 3

EXAMPLE OF CROP ROTATION

YEAR 1

Peas	Peas	Corn	Corn
Tomato	Tomato	Squash	Squash

YEAR 2

Squash	Squash	Peas	Peas
Corn	Corn	Tomato	Tomato

YEAR 3

Tomato	Tomato	Squash	Squash
Peas	Peas	Corn	Corn

YEAR 4

Corn	Corn	Tomato	Tomato
Squash	Squash	Peas	Peas

Green Manures

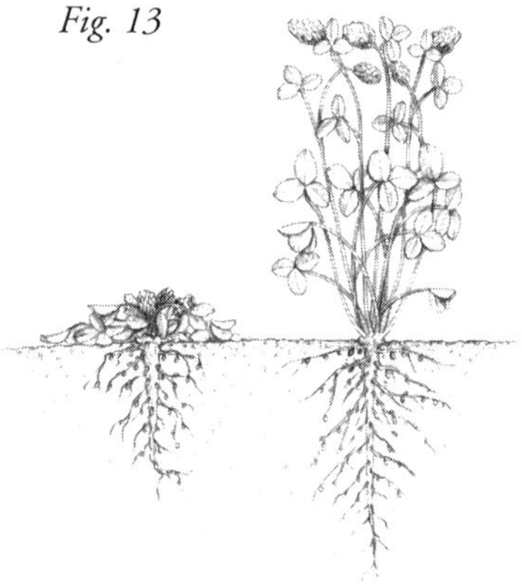

Many farm crops such as clover, alfalfa, and vetch can be rejuvenators for your garden soil. They will cover and protect unused areas and store nitrogen for future use. When planted specifically to take advantage of their soil-enhancing qualities, these plants are called green manures.

Farmers and gardeners since the beginning of agriculture have been aware that legumes can improve the soil for the following crop. But it wasn't until the late 1800s that science understood the mechanism involved. Specific soil bacteria live in association with the roots of legumes. Through this symbiotic (mutually beneficial) association, the bacteria provide the legumes with access to the nitrogen in the air, while the legume roots provide nutrition to the bacteria. The captured nitrogen is stored in nodules on the roots.

Fig. 13

Whether the legumes are turned under, killed by winter temperatures, or mowed and composted, the nodules remain in the soil for other plants to use. Since nitrogen is an important food, this natural process adds plant food to the soil. If you have not grown a specific legume in your garden before, I recommend that you purchase inoculant bacteria when you purchase the legume seeds. The inoculant comes in the form of a dry powder that looks like fine compost and contains the symbiotic bacteria specific to that legume. You mix the powder with the seeds before sowing. This is just one more example of how gardeners can work with the built-in processes of the natural world to enhance the fertility of their garden soil.

Nodules remain in the soil even after the legume dies.

You can sow legumes for green manure in any empty space in the garden. You can even sow them with the crop in anticipation of the bed becoming empty in the future. That practice is called *undersowing*. It is like planting a deliberate but noncompetitive weed. Most garden plants are sufficiently well established by a month after planting so that the competition of small plants underneath will not hinder them. In fact, you can even let the weeds grow after a month and still get a reasonable yield. Instead, I have learned to plant legumes as deliberate weeds.

About a month after I have established well-spaced crops such as broccoli, cabbage, corn, squashes, beans, and eggplant, I sprinkle the legume seeds on the soil under the crop and mix them in shallowly. The legume will grow in the understory of the crop. When the crop is harvested and the residues removed to the compost heap, a bed of green manure is already growing. Undersowing is a fun option. You get to grow the crop and initiate soil improvement simultaneously.

In general, green manures are planted like small patches of lawn. Broadcast the seeds on bare soil, rake them in, then tamp the soil lightly with the back of the rake to make sure the seeds are in contact with moist earth. You can do this anywhere you want a green manure as the next crop in the rotation, although it is not worth the trouble if it will be growing for less than 6 to 8 weeks. A green manure will protect the soil over the coming winter, shade it during a hot period between spring and fall crops, or help renovate the soil in a bed that needs some extra care.

Once you have grown a green manure, you have to bury or remove the greenery to obtain a clean seedbed for the next crop. You can incorporate the green manure residues by turning over the soil shallowly with a spade. If you do that, you should wait 3 weeks before planting or transplanting because the early stages of the decomposition process after residues are incorporated into the soil can inhibit seed germination and root growth. Alternatively, you can cut the crop off as close to the ground as possible and add the greenery to the compost heap. Then chop the surface clean with a hoe to prevent regrowth, rake the bed smooth, and spread a little compost on the surface. The bed is then ready for transplants or large seeds. Smaller seeds that need a finer seedbed may be at a slight disadvantage.

There is one other effortless system for managing green manures: freeze them out. This system will still protect the soil through the fall and winter but will save work the following spring. Choose your green manure cover crop from among those legumes that grow well in the cool weather of late summer, fall, and early winter but are not hardy enough to survive the winter in your area. Even though the plants are killed, the residues will protect the soil for the remainder of the winter. In spring, rake the bed clean and add the rakings to the compost heap, then you're ready to plant.

I have as much fun fitting green manure crops into the

garden plan, whether undersown or seeded on their own, as I do growing vegetables. Green manures are another part of the process. When the soil is not needed for human food, it makes sense to plant it to soil food. To benefit the soil of all the beds, you will want to move the green manure areas around the garden as part of your crop rotation. I prefer to sow legumes as green manures, but grasses such as rye, oats, and barley also are useful, especially before leguminous vegetables such as peas and beans. Mustard, oil radish, phacelia, and buckwheat are other non-leguminous green manures. Different green manures have particular uses in the garden, just as different vegetables have specific uses in the kitchen.

Rye, Oats, and Barley—Rye can be planted later in the fall than most other green manures and will grow a lot of bulk. It is hardy enough to survive the coldest winters. I don't use rye in my garden because it requires so much work to get rid of the

TABLE 4

GREEN MANURES

Legumes	Non-Legumes
HARDY	
Hairy vetch	Rye
Red clover	Wheat
Sweet clover	
White Dutch clover	
HALF-HARDY	
Austrian winter pea	Barley
Berseem clover	Mustard
Black Medic	Oats
Crimson clover	Oil radish
Lupine	Phacelia
Purple vetch	
Rose clover	
TENDER	
Cowpeas	Buckwheat
Crotolaria	
Guar	
Sesbania	

following spring. You have to spade it under thoroughly, or it will regrow. If you wish to use a grass family green manure, I suggest growing either an oat or barley variety that is not winter hardy in your region. This generally applies to gardeners in Zone 6 and north. Cleaning up the residues of winter-killed oats or barley is as simple as raking the surface clean—much easier than trying to get rye under control.

Buckwheat and Others—Although buckwheat will be killed by the slightest frost, it is useful during the summer to smother weeds on new ground. It grows quickly once the weather is warm, and its leaves rapidly shade out weed competition. You have to cut it down and turn it under or compost the residues once it begins to flower. If it sets seed and self-sows, buckwheat can become a weed in its own right.

British gardeners favor mustard as a fast-growing, short-term green manure (except before cabbage family relatives). They find that both its root structure and rapidly decomposed tops stimulate beneficial microorganisms in the soil. Any home-garden variety of mustard can be used. A Dutch favorite is phacelia *(Phacelia tanacetifolia),* originally a California weed. My Dutch friends regard it as one of the best all-around green manures and a real benefit to any subsequent crop. German gardeners often include oil radish in their green manures. It has a deep taproot that loosens the subsoil and is also reputed to have a beneficial effect on microorganisms. To my knowledge, neither phacelia nor oil radish seeds are easily available in the United States, but keep your eyes open.

Green manures will care for your garden when you can't. If travel or business calls you away for long periods of time in spring, summer, or fall, you can sow the whole garden to a soil-enhancing crop before you leave. The soil in a neglected garden will eventually cover itself with weeds or other wild vegetation unless you take action and plant your choice of "weed." Planting an intentional soil-improving cover crop will help keep out the unwanted weeds and make it much easier to resume gardening upon your return.

CHAPTER 4

THE OUTDOOR GARDEN: PLANTING AND CULTIVATING

*I*f compost is the life source of the garden, seeds are the life spark. I have always marveled that a carrot, bunch of celery, or cabbage could be hidden in such a tiny speck. Yet that small seed is a powerhouse of performance. Take the tomato, for example. Do you want return on investment? One tomato seed, yielding at least 1000 to 1 in 4 months, makes even the highest fliers seem paltry. Are you fascinated by design and miniaturization? The finest computer is but a crude makeshift device beside a tomato seed. How about impregnable packaging? Tomato seeds are known to remain viable through the most thorough waste-processing technologies and emerge unscathed to sprout all over the sludge heaps at sewage plants. To top it all off, if those seeds are sown in your well-composted home garden, the results will be equally impressive in flavor, tenderness, and eating satisfaction.

I purchase seeds principally through seed catalogs. I like the broad selection of old favorites, the yearly introduction of newcomers, and the prompt service. There are enough seed catalogs available to fit all climates and to fill the space limitations of a small pickup if you were to send for all of them. Be discriminating. Over the years, I have settled on 3 or 4 catalogs (see appendix) that allow me more than adequate climatic and culinary latitude without overwhelming me or my mailbox.

Seeds for the Four-Season Harvest

Since I intend to garden in four seasons, I have to plan ahead. When the seed catalogs arrive in midwinter, I don't procrastinate. I check the seed drawer in the cupboard to determine what's left from last year. If seeds are stored in a cool, dry location, I find I can count on them to be adequately viable the second year. Then I check my garden notes to see which ones I wished I had ordered more of, which new varieties were successful, and which varieties I decided to replace. Also in my notes are the fruits of observing the garden in action. Comments like "does much better in fall than spring" or "grew exceptionally well planted in clumps" are invaluable for future varietal selection.

Then I begin with the catalogs. Reordering the dependable standards is straightforward. Hunting for replacements requires more careful perusal. At times I may be seeking a specific virtue (a variety that stores longer or gives better hot-weather performance); at other times I would like to find a variety with superior adaptability to my soil conditions (some varieties do better in sandy soil, others in clay). Even if the catalog description doesn't specify the qualities I seek, I learn a lot by reading between the lines. For example, "drought-resistant" varieties often do well in sandy soil; "quick-growing" varieties will respond to extra compost, moisture, and warmth. At times I am simply tempted by a particularly enticing phrase: "exceptionally delicate flavor," "eye pleasing," "wonderful heirloom," "our personal favorite." I list my variety favorites for each vegetable in Chapter 9.

It is necessary to rein in the contagious enthusiasm of the moment and restrain yourself somewhat. The writers of seed catalog descriptions are a sales force, and we are all susceptible. You may suddenly find that your passion has created a monster of 2500 finely tuned varieties requiring a staff of 9 to manage. I avoid that by limiting myself, for the most part, to a single variety of each vegetable. So instead of buying seeds for a low-growing, very early pea, another with good flavor and lovely chartreuse blossoms, and another that is tall, late, and "highly recommended

Fig. 14

Seeds and catalogs

by Sir Cedric," I have settled on one dependable, very flavorful, long-yielding variety, such as *Lincoln*, and I enjoy both the vegetable and the ease of management.

Once I determine what and how much I need for the next year of gardening, I order promptly. Time, tide, and the garden wait for no one. All of a sudden, there may be an early thaw. You notice an empty space and have an opportunity to plant. Your inspiration, experience, or planting schedule tells you a specific seed variety could be planted at that moment. What comfort to know it's waiting in the seed drawer.

Sowing Seeds

Seeds are determined to grow. The gardener's role is to help them do so. The first step in plant growth is seed germination. Three factors that contribute to its success are soil temperature, seed depth, and moisture. If you have chosen and/or modified your garden site to enhance the microclimate, the outdoor soil temperature conditions will have been improved already. The other conditions, the depth at which the seeds are planted and the moisture level of the soil after planting, can be more directly controlled by the gardener.

Seeds are planted in either a hole in the soil or a furrow (a long, shallow opening) and then covered. The covering of soil keeps the seeds moist, warm, and protected while they germinate. As a general rule for depth of planting, I suggest covering a seed to 3 or 4 times its diameter. Thus, I cover a small seed, such as a carrot seed, which measures about 1/16-inch in diameter, with 1/4 inch of soil. I plant a 1/4-inch-diameter pea or corn seed 1 inch deep. In a heavy clay soil, the 3 times factor is more appropriate. As general rules go, this one is quite dependable for most garden seeds. If I sow large seeds, such as peas, beans, or corn, when the weather is warmer and drier than usual, I plant them slightly deeper to ensure adequate moisture for germination.

When planting small seeds, you can make accurate shallow furrows with the edge of a board. I use a 30-inch-long 1-by-2 for planting rows across the beds. I lay a sharp edge of the board on the soil where I want the furrow and wiggle it in a little to move the soil aside. When I lift the board up, it leaves a shallow, level, V-shaped furrow across the bed. I then drop in the seeds and

Fig. 15

Making a furrow with a board

cover them lightly by pushing soil over them with my fingers. For larger seeds, such as pea and bean, I make a furrow with the edge of a hoe. For corn and squash seeds, I poke a hole with my finger to the desired depth.

When you sprinkle the seeds in furrows, take the extra time to space them evenly. Aim for the distances suggested in Chapter 9. It is worth spacing seeds carefully. The thinning will be less destructive to the remaining plants if the plants are not tangled together. An easy way to sow is to crease one side of the seed packet and use the V of that crease to align the seeds as you tap them out one by one. With practice, this can be a very efficient technique. You also can use one of the small seed-sowing aids sold in seed catalogs, but in most cases, after fiddling and

Fig. 16

Sowing seeds with a creased seed packet

adjusting and refiddling with them, I usually decide that it is simpler to sow by hand.

Once you have planted the seeds at the proper depth, you must keep them moist. When the weather is dry, I water the seed rows daily until the seeds germinate. I make a quick pass using a watering can with a fine rose or a hose and sprinkler nozzle. This is especially important with small seeds, such as carrot and parsley seeds, that are planted shallowly and take a while to germinate. By watering those rows once or twice a day until the seedlings emerge, you can guarantee a full stand with no gaps in the row.

Transplanting

Transplanting is like seeding except that you set out young plants (seedlings) rather than seeds. Whether you acquire the seedlings by purchasing them from a garden center or growing your own, the techniques for moving them to the garden are the same.

Fig. 17

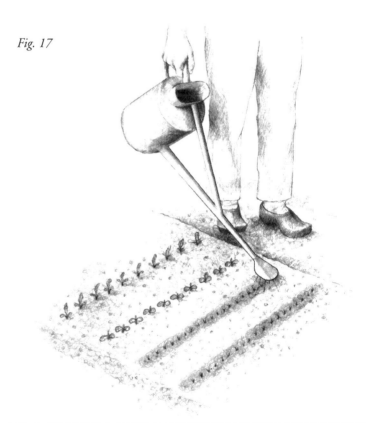

Water daily until seedlings begin to emerge.

(Information on growing your own seedlings is given in Chapter 5.) Before transplanting, I make sure the soil around the seedling roots is very moist. That is their best protection against the stress of drying out while they are becoming established. After they are in the ground, I water the whole bed. Within a few days, they start rooting out into the soil around them and are then like any other plant in the garden.

To reduce the effort of measuring and spacing the transplants, I use homemade marking jigs. These are lightweight wooden frames the width of the bed and 3 to 4 feet long. They have pegs screwed in at the spacing I want for the plants. When I press the frame and pegs against the prepared soil, the pegs leave marks. I then make a hole and set a transplant at each mark. The spacing is automatic.

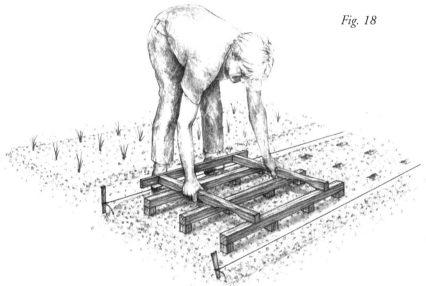

Fig. 18

Homemade marking jig

I find a standard garden trowel uncomfortable to use when making holes for small transplants because of the strain it places on the wrist. I prefer a transplant tool that allows me to jab and pull with my wrist straight. There is an excellent design on the market called the Right-Angle trowel (see appendix), or you can make your own tool by following the instructions in the next paragraph.

Purchase a bricklayer's trowel with a triangular blade (2 by

Fig. 19

Transplanting tool

5 inches) and a strong attachment between the handle and blade. Use a hacksaw to cut 2 inches off the end of the blade. Clamp a vise firmly just above where the handle meets the blade. Bend the handle back until it is parallel with the blade and then a few degrees farther. You hold the resulting tool like a dagger. Just jab it into the soil, then pull it back toward you, and you will have a hole the right size for your transplant.

Trellised Crops

I fit many space-demanding crops into my 30-inch-wide beds by growing them vertically. Climbing peas, pole beans, and tomatoes all benefit from trellises for vertical support. Trellises are not a garden necessity but a choice. You should not feel any obligation to trellis your crops if it seems too complicated. All vegetable crops can be grown without support. Just be sure to choose low-growing varieties. For example, *Sugar Snap* and *Alderman* peas grow 6 feet tall and need support, but other varieties with vines under 30 inches (such as *Daybreak* or *Knight*) can be grown on the ground. The seed catalog description gives that information. With beans, choose bush varieties over pole varieties if you don't plan to stake them. Similarly, there are varieties of bush cucumbers and bush squashes if you don't have enough space for trailing vines. Tomatoes for ground culture should be determinate rather than indeterminate (see Chapter 9). Again, catalog descriptions will inform you.

For those of you who, like me, are intrigued by the idea of trellises, you can grow many trellised crops in addition to peas, beans, and tomatoes. Among these are cucumbers, melons, winter squashes and even a vining zucchini and New Zealand spinach that can all be grown vertically. The advantages of trellising are numerous: 2 to 3 times higher yields from the same garden space, more efficient use of sunlight for optimal photosynthesis, easier picking with no bending over, and cleaner produce because there is no soil splatter from rain or watering.

I build the same basic trellis for all vertically growing crops. It consists of upright poles every 7 ½ feet with a crossbar on top. You can use poles cut in the woods or 2-by-2s from the lumberyard. A standard 2-by-4 ripped lengthwise will yield a pair of 2-by-2s. I don't use treated wood for this trellis because

I prefer not to be around the chemicals it is treated with. You can apply an environmentally friendly wood preservative yourself. (See appendix.) If you have access to a scrap yard, you can make this simple trellis out of metal pipe.

The uprights are 8 feet long, and I sharpen them to a point for driving into the ground. I place a pole at either end of the 15-foot-long beds and another in the center. In my sandy soil, I drive the poles 1½ to 2 feet deep for solid support. That leaves 6 feet or so aboveground. If you make a preliminary hole with an iron bar, it will be much easier to drive the poles. In heavier soils that provide support, you can cut the uprights shorter and not drive them in as deep.

The crossbar is a 15-foot 2-by-2 that sits on the 3 uprights. I drill a 7/32-inch hole through the crossbar and into the top of the upright. Then I drop a galvanized 20d nail in the hole to hold the crossbar in place. This makes a simple, attractive structure that

Fig. 20

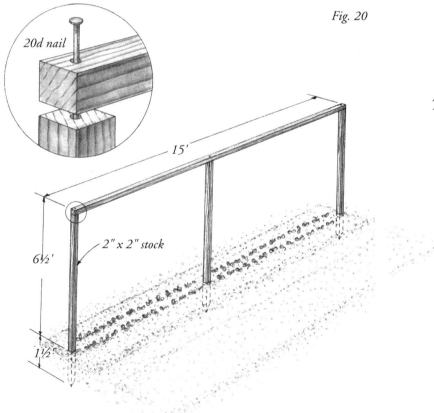

20d nail

15'

2" x 2" stock

6½'

1½'

The trellis frame

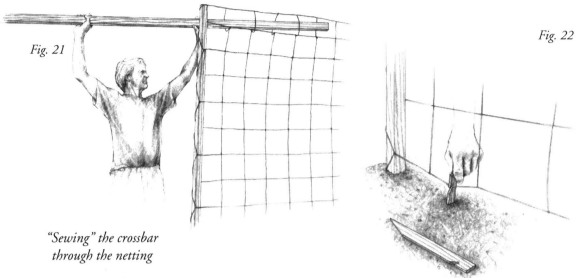

Fig. 21

Fig. 22

"Sewing" the crossbar through the netting

Right: Securing the netting with a notched peg

will not blow over and is strong enough to support the weight of the crop. It needs to be strong. You may be surprised by how many pounds of fruit are carried by a row of trellised beefsteak tomatoes.

I settled on a 6-foot height because that was the height of the tallest pea netting I could find. The best pea netting is made of nylon or plastic and has a large mesh with 6-inch-square holes (see appendix for sources). I hang the mesh from the crossbar by "sewing" the crossbar through alternate holes in the top edge of the mesh. Then I place the crossbar on top of the uprights and drop in the nails. I drive garden stakes (1 inch square and 12 inches long) with a slight notch near the upper end to hold the netting taut at the bottom. This is the simplest, strongest, and most versatile trellis I have ever used.

I use trellis netting as the climbing support for peas, cucumbers, melons, squash, vining zucchini, and New Zealand spinach. I use untreated garden twine for tomatoes and pole beans. The 4- or 5-ply strength is best. Tie the twine to the crossbar and then down to a garden stake driven into the soil next to the tomato plant or hill of beans. The beans will climb the string on their own. Prune the tomatoes to one stem and support them by taking a turn of the string around the stem every so often as it grows. That provides enough friction between string and stem to hold the plants upright. At the end of the season, compost the string with the vines. (See Chapter 9 for more detailed pruning and tying instructions for tomatoes.)

This same trellis frame will support a sheet of plastic to make a temporary A-frame greenhouse to protect your tomatoes into the first cool weeks of autumn. Bury the edges of the plastic in the soil of the path on each side. Close in the ends by clipping with clothespins. This temporary structure will not protect against strong winds but will provide an excellent level of frost protection.

You can leave the uprights in the ground permanently if you wish. You would then rotate the trellised crops to a different trellised bed each year. Actually, you can grow any crop you want in a trellised bed. If you remove the crossbar, the 3 uprights cast almost no shade and are not in the way of planting, harvesting, or using the broadfork. If you plan to leave the uprights in place permanently, the wood should be a rot-resistant species such as cedar or coated with one of the environmentally friendly wood preservatives. If you remove them at the end of the season, dry them, and store them under cover, they will last many years with no preservative.

Fig. 23

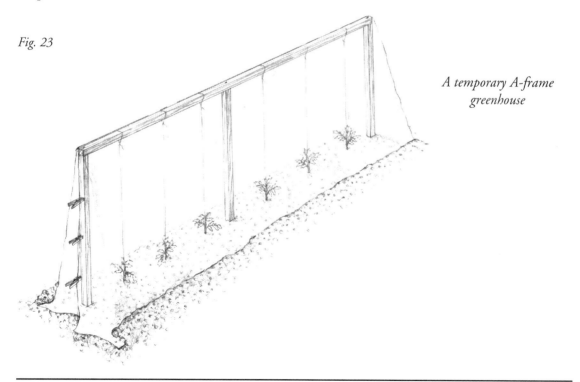

A temporary A-frame greenhouse

Weeds

I suspect that weeds probably discourage more potential garden-ers than any other single problem. "Oh, the garden was so overgrown with weeds that we finally gave up" is so common a statement that it is almost considered a normal reaction. It doesn't need to be that way. I have never heard anyone say, "Oh, the living room finally got so dirty that we just stopped using it." We don't stop enjoying the living room because of dust. We simply vacuum or sweep every so often to keep the room clean. The same applies in the garden. Furthermore, just as dirt in the living room can be minimized by placing a mat outside the front door or asking people to remove their shoes before entering the house, weeds in the garden can be prevented in a number of ways. All of them make less work for the gardener.

First, don't dig the garden. Let buried seeds stay buried. Most weed seeds germinate only in the top 2 inches of soil. When starting a new garden, you can encourage that germination by shallow rotary tilling. The mixture of air, moisture, and exposure to light creates conditions that stimulate weed germination. Wait a week after tilling and till again to eradicate all the newly germinated weeds before you plant. Once the upper-layer weed seeds are exhausted (it takes a number of years, so be patient), very few new weeds will appear unless you bring them up from below or you don't pay attention to my next suggestion.

Don't let weeds go to seed. Nature is prolific. Each plant can produce an enormous number of seeds. The old saying "One year's seeding means seven year's weeding" holds. You won't get any debate from me, because I have seen it. The results of carelessness are cumulative: the more seeds you have, the more weeds you have. But the results of care also are cumulative. If weed plants are removed from the garden to the compost heap before they go to seed, their thousands of seeds are not added to the garden lode: no seeds, no weeds. As the years progress, there will be fewer and fewer seeds left to germinate. Of course, your life will be even easier if you follow my final suggestion.

Dispatch weeds while they are small. Tiny, newly germinated weeds are the easiest to deal with. A sharp hoe drawn shallowly through the soil between the crop rows will quickly dispatch small weeds. That minimum effort yields a maximum benefit. It not only cures the weed problem but also makes the garden look neat and cared for. Because it looks nice, you will spend more quiet and relaxed time there keeping it that way. This is not weeding, which is work, but rather cultivating. Cultivating is the gentle, shallow stirring of the soil's surface that uproots newly germinated weeds before they become a problem.

If a hoe is to be effective when "drawn shallowly through the soil," that hoe must be sharp; angled for drawing, not chopping; slim, so as not to bulldoze soil onto the vegetable plants; and accurate, so as to pass between the crop rows without damage. It also must be comfortable and fun to use, or you will find some other way to spend your time. I could never find such a hoe, so I made my own. Let me explain the process.

I was after a draw hoe, not a chopping hoe. I wanted an efficiently designed tool, not a crude bludgeon. I wanted a hoe I could use standing upright (no back strain) and draw toward me shallowly just under the soil's surface. Since that meant I would be holding it with my thumbs up the handle, as with a broom or leaf rake, I had to find the ideal angle between the blade

Fig. 24

The gardener with a draw, or collineal hoe. Note hand position.

Fig. 25

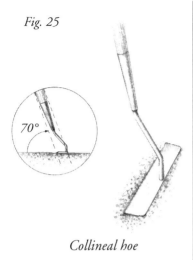

Collineal hoe

Fig. 26

Stirrup hoe

and the handle for a shallow, skimming action. Seventy degrees turned out to be ideal. I made the blade as thin and narrow as possible so that it would cut and skim without gouging and bulldozing. Since the blade was narrow, I could put the cutting edge in line with the centerline of the hoe handle so that it could be aimed accurately and cut weeds rather than crops. Finally, I sharpened it like a razor so that the cutting edge was next to the soil. A sharp hoe allows you to work shallowly and not disturb the roots of the crop plants. Voilà, the hoe of my dreams.

Using a draw hoe with the proper angle and a thin, sharp blade is like dancing with a skilled partner, and just as enjoyable. Hold it in a ballroom-dancing position, with your thumbs upward. Stand comfortably with your back straight. The hoe blade draws effortlessly through the soil of the growing areas. This is a very pleasant activity. Hoe when weeds are very small, keeping the garden shallowly cultivated. Go out to the garden on a summer's evening, put a Strauss waltz on the stereo, and dance with your hoe. Weed control has never been so civilized.

Your evening dancing partner is called the collineal hoe (collineal means "in the same straight line"). Various interpretations of this design are sold by a number of garden tool catalogs. It is designed for skimming in soft, fertile soil rather than for chopping compacted earth. The only compaction in your garden should be in the paths. For those areas, another hoe will make your life easier.

This is called a stirrup hoe because it has a thin, curved blade held by a square frame somewhat in the shape of a stirrup. The stirrup is hinged where it attaches to the handle so it swings back and forth slightly. The blade is sharpened on both edges. The hinged action changes the angle of the blade to the soil just enough so that it cuts smoothly whether you are pushing or pulling. This hoe is held with the thumbs pointing down the handle so that a lot of power can be applied. It can cut effectively just below the soil's surface or go deeper if you wish. The cutting blade is curved and fits nicely in the paths between the beds where your feet have passed. I use this hoe while moving down the paths backward, working the hinged action of the hoe back and forth in the compacted soil. It neatly cuts off all weeds and leaves a fresh, aerated surface.

Fig. 27

The gardener with a stirrup hoe

Garden Friends

Before we leave the outdoor garden, I have one final suggestion. I realize this is unconventional in a gardening book, but I'd like to introduce you to a delightful garden helper. Back in the fifties, cartoonist Al Capp created the Schmoo, a roly-poly little creature that inhabited his Li'l Abner comic strip. Schmoos were friendly animals who provided all manner of food and services willingly and joyfully to the inhabitants of Dogpatch. I think there is a real-life Schmoo that might interest gardeners. This creature can provide you with a daily source of fresh eggs, devastatingly effective slug control, and charming garden companionship. The real-life backyard Schmoo is the duck.

I became interested in ducks because I enjoy eating eggs as fresh as my vegetables. Chickens are not my preference because they are a little too rowdy. Their gallinaceous behavior, always scratching, fighting, or taking dust baths, is destructive in a garden. They also require special food and upscale housing.

Fig 28

The real-life Schmoo in the garden

Ducks are a much better choice. They lay more eggs than chickens, and the eggs are richer and better tasting—great as omelets. Furthermore, ducks lay at night, so the eggs are always waiting for you the next morning. Morning-laying chickens are wont to lay their eggs surreptitiously in inaccessible places. Best of all, ducks lay eggs at a reasonable rate during the winter without fancy housing or supplementary light. Even if fed on a homegrown diet of garden and kitchen scraps, instead of the expensive mixed feeds that chickens require, ducks will lay at about 60 percent of the normal rate. They need water only for drinking, not swimming, although they do appreciate the water from a sprinkler in hot, dry weather, just as the garden does.

If you plant a home orchard next to your garden, you have the perfect situation for ducks. Whether you keep a pair (they like company) or more, you can house them in a small night shelter in the orchard. Whenever you wish, you can fence them into selected areas of the garden for slug control. Or you can fence a grassy track around the garden as a duck run. The ducks will quietly patrol the perimeter, grazing on grass and dining happily on any slugs that try to cross their path as if they had been trained to the task. Web-footed guards armed with a voracious appetite are the most dependable, environmentally sound slug control any gardener could desire.

CHAPTER 5

THE COVERED GARDEN:
COLD FRAMES

I t is the middle of January on the coast of Maine, and I'm harvesting crops for dinner. Despite the typically frigid New England weather, I can choose from 18 garden-fresh vegetables. I begin by harvesting a salad of mâche, curly endive, and claytonia. (See Chapter 9 for specific information on these and other hardy crops.) I will serve the salad with a mustard vinaigrette and raw carrot and kohlrabi slices on the side. Then I gather spinach for a duck-egg soufflé, dig some leeks to prepare sautéed with butter, and pick some parsley to garnish the potatoes from the cellar. Planning ahead, I decide to have sorrel soup; an arugula, radicchio, and sugarloaf salad with fresh scallions; and steamed brussels sprouts in a mornay sauce for tomorrow night. The menu also could include au gratin Swiss chard, braised escarole, a cream of kale and potato soup, or dandelion-hearts tempura. Not bad for fresh garden harvesting in Zone 5.

Shifting from chef to gardener, I notice a few empty spaces where I harvested crops earlier in the winter. I take some seed packets from my pocket and make my first early-spring plantings of radishes, arugula, mizuna, spinach, and three varieties of lettuce. Germination will be slow, but they will be off and growing in a month or so as winter retreats. Nearby is a bed of

September-sown lettuce plants that will be ready to eat by early March. Outdoor beds of parsnips should be ready to dig later that month.

Yes, this really is Zone 5, where the average low temperature is -10° to -20°F and the ground is frozen from December to March. I enjoyed similar winter harvests when I lived in Zone 3. I haven't done a lot of extra garden work to be able to eat this well. I planted all these crops during the summer and early fall. I provided them with protective covers once the cool weather arrived. That slight protection allows me to harvest them all winter long. You will notice that none of the crops I've mentioned are the typical heat lovers of the summer garden. And therein lies the secret.

Other times and cultures knew the gardening and eating delights of the traditional cold-weather crops. The ingredients in the cuisine reflected the time of year. But since the advent of modern transportation, when the warm-weather crops are no longer available locally, we purchase them from other regions. That situation has limited not only our diet but also our thinking about growing winter foods.

When the energy crisis of the early 1970s focused attention on extended-season production in northern areas, the solar designers directed most of their efforts toward extending the growing season for warm-weather crops. They never questioned the dietary assumption of a perpetual summer. The systems they developed emphasized the free heat from the sun—how to capture and store it. Consequently, their structures were complex, dependent on space-age materials, and, although technologically ingenious, horticulturally limited. Much of the expense and a high proportion of the protected space were devoted to storing heat for warm-weather crops.

Because I am a gardener, not an engineer, I look for more natural solutions. A slight moderation of the climate is all that's necessary for hardy plants to thrive. Thus I am not going to discuss heat pumps, thermal mass, solar gain, or R factors because they are too complicated. They make the simple joys of food production seem more industrial than poetic. Given the option, I prefer poetry. I take my design clues from the natural world, where simple systems with biological diversity are the most successful and enduring.

Crop Protection

In much of the continental United States we need to moderate the winter climate to be able to harvest a variety of winter foods, because our normal weather is harsher and more changeable than the cold but more evenly tempered regions where many of these plants originated. We don't need to provide warmth. In fact, too warm temperatures can be detrimental. But we do need to take the edge off the harshness of sudden change. There is an old saying in New England that if you don't like the weather, just wait 5 minutes. I have often seen a rainy day with a temperature of 55°F during a midwinter thaw change to a clear, cold night with strong winds and a -5°F thermometer reading. Such extremes are true for much of the country.

Hardy plants don't mind cold, but they are affected by those alternating freeze/thaw, wet/dry, and gale/calm conditions. Such extremes are as stressful to plants as they are to humans. The aim of crop protection in the winter garden is to lessen those climatic extremes and consequently lessen plant stress. The first step toward lessening plant stress is to cover the plants. The simplest cover is a cold frame.

The Magic Box

Gardeners should dedicate a monument to the cold frame. It is the simplest, most flexible, and most successful low-tech tool for modifying the garden climate. It's simple because it is basically a box with a glass top and no bottom that sits on the soil. It's flexible because it can be made as long, as wide, or as tall as the gardener wishes. And it's successful because it is a tried-and-true garden aid that has been used in one form or another since ancient times (sheets of mica predated glass). The cold frame was the foundation for the early development of intensive commercial horticulture.

My first experience with cold frames came when I was a child, long before I began growing plants. A gardening neighbor had a small cold frame in which she grew hardy flowers for early and late blooms. I can remember going over to her yard every so often to see the "magic box." The drab tones of fall and winter prevailed in the outdoor world, but inside the frame, a riot of bright colors and green leaves existed. It was like looking into a warm, friendly house on a cold, snowy night. I never knew what flowers she grew in there—possibly calendulas and chrysanthemums, strawflowers and anemones—but their beauty stuck in my memory. I experience that same fascination today when I look into the green and growing world of my vegetable cold frames. The magic is created with a single sheet of glass and the careful selection of hardy cultivars.

How the Cold Frame Works

The cold frame lessens climatic stress in a number of ways:

Temperature. A single layer of glass creates a microclimate in which the nighttime temperature inside the frame can be as much as 20°F warmer than the temperature outside, although the average difference is 7° to 10°F. The daytime temperature inside the frame, even on a cloudy, early-spring day, will be 10° to 15°F warmer than outdoors. On a sunny day, the temperature can rise high enough to cook the soil and the plants if you don't vent off the extra heat. Both daytime and nighttime temperature differences depend on the time of year, the angle and intensity of the sun, the rate of outdoor temperature change, and the initial temperature in the frame.

Moisture. Much of the havoc that freezing can wreak on winter vegetables is a function of how wet the plants are. A plant just soaked by a rainstorm before freezing will be more stressed than one that is dry. The glass roof of the cold frame protects the crops inside from excess moisture.

Wind. The wind can make a cool day feel very cold. Weather forecasters always mention the windchill factor. The same conditions affect plants. Wind cools by removing ambient heat and evaporating moisture. The stress of winter wind alone can mean the difference between life and death for hardy vegetables. Even the slightest windbreak will help. One fall I planted two beds of spinach to winter over outdoors. I covered one lightly with a mulch of pine boughs and left the other uncovered. Even though

I could look through the thin layer of pine boughs and clearly see the spinach, that minimal amount of wind protection was significant. Ninety-five percent of the protected spinach survived the winter, compared to five percent of the unprotected crop.

Building the Cold Frame

A cold frame is basically a bottomless box that sits on the soil and has a glass cover. Thus, there are two parts—the sides (the box) and the top (the glass).

The sides can be made of almost any material—boards, concrete blocks, bales of hay, logs, and so on, all of which have their virtues. From my experience, I suggest making the sides out of boards. This will give you a frame that is long lasting, easy to construct, easy to use, reasonably light, and movable.

The top covering is called a *light*. In the old days, lights were 4 to 6 feet square and made of overlapping panes of glass. They were heavy and required two people to carry them. Today's home gardeners often use old storm windows as lights. Storm windows are easy to find and the size is right for covering cold frames. Modern lights can be glazed with translucent materials other than glass, such as plastic, polycarbonate, or fiberglass. Depending on its size, a cold frame is covered with one or more lights.

A cold frame can be any width that the lights will cover and any length or height. Traditional home garden cold frames measure 4 to 6 feet front to back and are 8 to 12 feet long. They are laid out with the long dimension running east to west. The frame should be just tall enough to clear the crops you plan to grow. In the standard design, the back wall is 12 inches high and the front wall 8 inches high, so that there is a slight slope to the south.

I have seen frames with the lights at a 45° angle facing south to maximize midwinter sun input. Such frames don't work as well as the traditional low-angle models for two reasons. First, you don't need maximum heat in midwinter for hardy crops. All they require is the protection of the frame. Second, there seems to be some benefit to having the glass roof near the plants as if it were a covering of snow. The environment inside the traditional low-angle frames better meets the needs of hardy crops.

The Cold Frame Box

Any cold frame design that protects the plants will serve you well. If you are going to enjoy using it, however, the design must be simple, attractive, pleasant to work with, and dependable. Having tried them all, I settled on the traditional design. My cold frames are rectangular wooden boxes, 8 feet long and 4 feet front to back, with a slight slope to the south. I build them out of 2-inch lumber to make them strong, but I think 1-inch stock would be adequate. Three 8-foot boards are necessary: 2 boards 12 inches wide and 1 board 8 inches wide. One of the 12-inch-wide boards is used for the back wall. The 8-inch-wide board is used for the front wall. The second 12-inch-board is cut into two 4-foot pieces, which are each cut diagonally lengthwise so that they are 8 inches wide at one end and 12 inches wide at the other.

I put the frame together with the boards sitting on a flat surface and the diagonal cut edge of the side walls facing up. When you do this, you will notice that the bottom edge of the frame is flat, whereas the upper edge has a slight discontinuity where the diagonal cut meets the front and back walls. For the lights to sit on the flattest surface, I turn the frame over before

*Construction of the
cold frame box*

Fig. 29

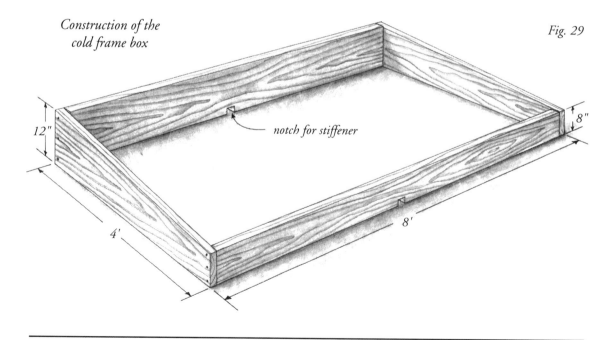

12"

notch for stiffener

8"

4'

8'

Fig. 30

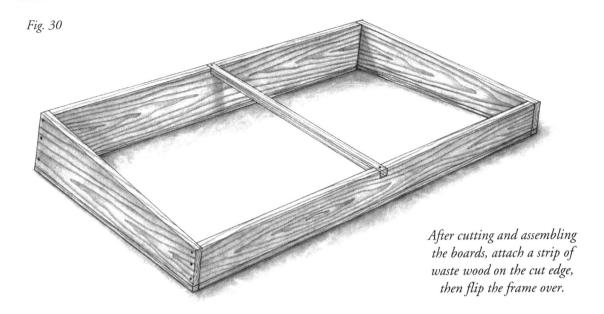

After cutting and assembling the boards, attach a strip of waste wood on the cut edge, then flip the frame over.

using it. Any discontinuity of the other edge is then hidden by contact with the soil. The frame will slant slightly to the south, allowing more light to enter.

I attach a 4-foot-long 2-by-2 to what is now the top. This piece extends across the middle of the frame, running front to back. This helps keep the sides spaced and also provides a handle that one person can use to lift the empty frame and carry it to a new location. If you use 1-inch wood, you might want to place more of these stiffeners across the frame.

I use standard pine or spruce for my frames. I purposely do not use treated wood, nor do I treat my frames with a preservative. I do not think that even the eco-products should be used in close proximity to food crops. Wood rots where it is in contact with the earth, however, so I attach a strip of scrap wood about 1 inch thick to the bottom edge of the frame where it touches the soil. In a few years, when this strip begins to rot, I replace it with another. The rest of the untreated wood frame will last for many years.

I also do not paint the frame. If I painted the interior white, it might reflect a little more light than the gray weathered wood, but paint is just one more complication. I would then have to scrape and paint every few years. I prefer to keep things simple.

The Cold Frame Light

The light sits on top of the frame like a cover on a pan. If it is glazed with plastic or another lightweight material, you will want to use clips or hooks and eyes to hold it on when the wind blows. The advantage of lights glazed with glass is that they are heavy enough not to be blown off under most conditions. If your garden is in a particularly windy spot, you may still want to take precautions. The simplest method is to fasten a raised border around the outside of the frame so that the wind can't catch under the edge of the light.

For many years, the lights covering my frames were 60-by-36-inch storm windows that I purchased on sale at the local lumberyard. They had been made to that size for a special order, but the customer never picked them up. Many home gardeners use storm windows as lights. They shouldn't be hard to find. Check the Yellow Pages or classified ads for salvage yards, distress sales, or old farm auctions where glass windows might be available. Companies that install aluminum storm windows might give you the names of customers who want to get rid of their old wooden storms.

I would still be using my old storm windows if I had not seen an even better design for lights on a trip to Holland in 1976. Glass cold frames were a traditional feature of Dutch commercial horticulture. Recently, they have almost died out in favor of huge greenhouses, but I was fortunate to visit an old-time market garden that still used this traditional technology. The feature that caught my eye was the simplicity of the Dutch lights. They were made specifically for cold frame use and avoided the problems that arise with storm windows.

Storm windows are meant to be used in a vertical position. When used horizontally, as on a cold frame, the wooden crossbars that hold the panes inhibit the flow of water off the frame. The trapped water can weaken and rot the crossbars and loosen the putty that holds the glass in place. As the putty deteriorates, the lights may drip water on the crops below.

The Dutch lights are designed for horticultural use. They consist of a simple wooden rim, approximately 2½ by 5 feet, with slots on the inside edges into which a single pane of glass is inserted. A small wooden stop at each end prevents the glass from sliding out. With the exception of the small stops, there are no crosspieces above the glass surface and thus nothing to inhibit the free flow of water. No putty is used, since the glass is held by the slots in the frame. I have always been fascinated with simple systems and with making them even better and simpler. The Dutch design for lights is a classic example.

Hemlock was the wood traditionally used for framing the lights. I make my light frames out of Maine white cedar. Any good western cedar, southern yellow pine, or spruce also should be suitable. The lights are not in contact with the earth. If carefully stored when not in use, they will last a long time.

Although the traditional Dutch lights are 5 by 2½ feet, I know from experience they are a little too heavy for many people to handle without practice. Therefore, I suggest that most home gardeners make them smaller, say 2 by 4 feet. My cold frames are separate from my 30-inch-wide garden beds, so their size is not contingent on garden layout. If I wished to use them to cover the 30-inch-wide beds, I would make the frames and lights to fit those dimensions. Conversely, if you already have some 36-inch-wide storm windows and wish to use them in the garden, you could make your garden beds 36 inches wide.

To construct Dutch lights, you will need 4 pieces of wood to make the rim that holds the glass. Let's say you wish to make the lights 2 by 4 feet. The two sides (each 4 feet long) are made from 2-by-2 stock (actual dimensions 1½-by-1½). A slot ¾ inch deep, cut with a table saw (called a kerf) runs the length of each piece. Make that cut 1 inch above what will be the bottom edge of these side rails. The 2 ends of the wooden rim are cut from a 2-by-2 to an actual dimension of 1-by-1½. They are 21 inches long. They hold the rails apart and support the glass at either end. I attach them at the corners with 4-inch galvanized drywall screws. The finished wooden rim of the light has outside dimensions of 2 by 4 feet.

The glass for that light is a single pane measuring 46½ by 22¾ inches. It slides into the kerfs in the side rails and rests on top of the end pieces. (You need to determine beforehand whether the kerf made by the saw blade is wide enough to accommodate the edge of the glass. If not, run the side piece through the saw again at a slightly different setting to widen it.)

The glass quality should be *double strength*. The glass I use also has been tempered. Tempered glass is more expensive but is 10 times more resistant to breakage. Attach a small piece of wood measuring ¾ by ½ by 3 inches in the middle of each end piece as a stop to hold the glass in place.

If glass breakage is a major concern for you or tempered glass seems too expensive, you could use one of the rigid greenhouse covering materials such as Lexan or Polygal. You can purchase these double-layer glass substitutes from greenhouse suppliers and cut them to size with a saw. The two layers are held apart by internal ribs. From an end view, they look like many square tubes glued side by side. If you use these materials for Dutch lights, you will need to cut a wider kerf into the side pieces, as these materials are thicker than double-strength glass.

Almost any of these options, and others yet to be conceived, will work for you. If you can find good storm windows, use them. If you can't and are fascinated, as I am, with simple design, you can build lights according to the Dutch model. Or you can purchase one of the many cold frames sold by garden catalogs. If you are more ingenious still, you will come up with an even better and simpler design and pioneer the next step in cold frame development. The evolution of this classic horticultural technology has resulted from the ideas of gardeners in the past and will continue through the inspiration of gardeners in the future.

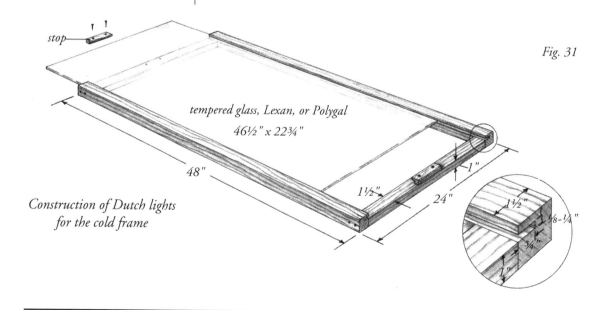

Fig. 31

stop

tempered glass, Lexan, or Polygal
46½" x 22¾"

48"

1½"

1"

24"

⅛–¼"

1½"

¾"

1"

*Construction of Dutch lights
for the cold frame*

Managing the Cold Frame

Successful cold frame management hinges on two practices: *temperature control* and *watering*. The amount of either that you have to do depends on the time of year.

Temperature control in a cold frame involves venting excess heat out the top. That can be done for you automatically during the winter months by equipping each frame with a temperature-activated opening arm (see appendix). The small amount of winter overheating can easily be vented by using one arm per frame, meaning that only one light opens. These mechanical helpers use a heat-activated pressure cylinder that expands with enough force to lift up to 20 pounds. If you want to use them, you will need to glaze your lights with one of the glass substitutes mentioned earlier. Lights glazed with glass are usually too heavy for the force that the cylinder can exert.

During the spring and fall, when the sun is higher in the sky, more venting will be necessary. Unless you want to purchase an automatic arm for each light on the frame, you will have to do a little hand work at those times of year. I use notched props to hold the lights open. I prop up the sides of the lights rather than the ends, and I angle the lights away from the prevailing winds. This gives the frame a sawtooth pattern and allows more even venting front to back. Early in the spring or late in the fall, you may need only one light open on the lowest notch on the prop. If I want a tiny bit of ventilation, I may slightly open the top edge of just one light per frame. Opening more lights or setting the prop at a higher notch increases the venting.

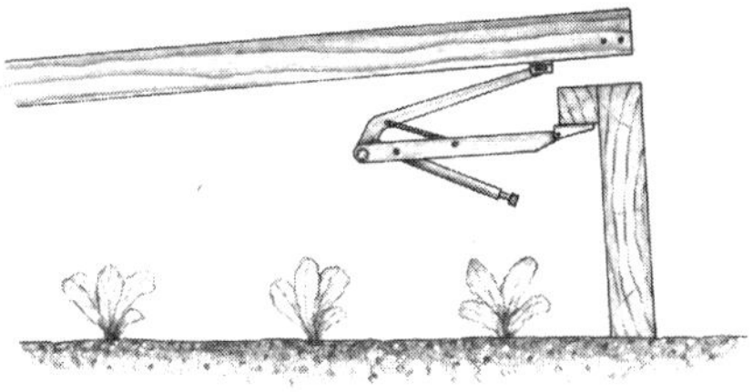

Keep a thermometer in the frame to give you some idea of the temperature. For the most accurate temperature readings, place the thermometer in a small, white slatted box that sits on the soil in the center of the frame. In this protected site, the thermometer will measure ambient air temperature rather than the direct effect of the sun's rays.

On sunny days, venting is an open-and-shut job. On rainy days, it is not necessary. On cloudy days, be sure to check the thermometer, as a lot of the sun's rays can come through clouds. I go out in the morning after the sun has risen sufficiently. Depending on the weather and my past experience, I prop the lights

Fig. 32

Automatic venting arm

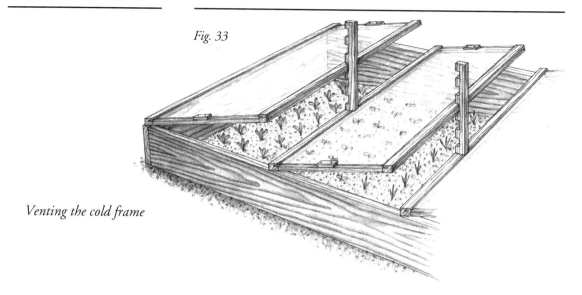

Fig. 33

Venting the cold frame

open as much as I think will be necessary. I aim for a 70°F temperature inside the frame in spring and 60° to 65°F in fall. I return in late afternoon, when the sun is no longer a major source of heat, and close them again. If I'm home and the weather changes dramatically during the day, I take whatever action is appropriate. When I'm gone all day, whether sunny or cloudy, I vent more than necessary in case the sun gets stronger.

The amount of venting depends on the season. In winter, you hardly have to vent at all; in fall, you vent progressively less; in spring, you vent progressively more. On average for Zone 5 and north, the line between the fall and winter cold frame seasons is around November 1. The line between the winter and spring seasons falls around February 15. In Zones 6 and 7, the dates are a little later in the fall and a little earlier in the spring. In the real icebox sections of the country, the winter period can begin as early as October 15 and last until March 1. I have grown hardy crops over the winter in one of the coldest parts of New England, and there the frames never needed venting for 4 months, 2 months on either side of the winter solstice. Whenever I opened the frames to harvest during the winter, the plants got all the air exchange they needed.

The seasonal transition takes place over a remarkably short time span for much of the country, since the determining factor is the effect of the sun rather than the temperature of the air. As the days shorten, the sun's path is lower in the sky and there is less solar radiation to heat up the frames. Once the sun's path is low enough, there is a period of about 3 months (6 weeks before the winter solstice and 6 weeks after it) when the gardener's only work is harvesting the bounty. The farther north you go, the longer this period becomes.

I call this 3- to 4-month season the Persephone months. In Greek mythology, the nongrowing season (the low-sun months of winter) was explained by the myth of Persephone. Persephone, daughter of the earth goddess Demeter, was loved by Hades, who abducted her to the netherworld. Demeter, with the help of Zeus, managed to get her back, but in the bargain, Persephone had to spend a third of the year with Hades. During those months, Demeter went into mourning and nothing grew. The Persephone months are when the cold frame crops reign supreme.

The cold season begins with the first warning of frost in the coldest areas and with the advent of cool nights farther south. At this point, the lights, which have been stored away all summer, are put back on the frames. The frames need to be well vented during the day (use the upper notches on the props) and closed only on nights that threaten a frost. As the season advances and temperatures decline, you will be venting less and closing the frames up slightly earlier in the day. Be conscious of Indian summer, which brings warmer temperatures, and vent accordingly.

The ideal is to keep the crops growing steadily in this protected environment but not to overheat them. With cold frames, it is always better to err on the cool side and vent the frames excessively rather than run them too warm. Very cold conditions are inevitable as winter arrives, and the soft, succulent tissues of plants that have been grown at too high temperatures will not be as hardy. A 65°F daytime temperature in the frame is a good target to aim for early in the fall. Reduce your goal to 60°F later on.

Once winter arrives the system is basically dormant. Your winter food is not dependent on sunny weather for warmth because it is already grown. You don't want to create summer conditions. In fact, on sunny winter days, you will be glad to vent off extra heat. Cloudy days with frame temperatures in the 30s and 40s are fine. The cold nights are no problem, since the winter food plants don't mind freezing. As long as the temperature in the frame gets above freezing every few days so the plants can thaw naturally before you harvest, all will be well.

Winter Cold Frame Crops

As the fall advances, the crops in the frames change. First are the crops for fall consumption. These were planted during the summer and covered with lights once the cool weather began. I harvest many of the same crops from the outdoor garden until they are ready in the frames. In Table 5, I give approximate planting dates for Zone 5. Consult Table 14, Planting Dates for an Extended Harvest, to adjust these dates for your area. For further information on specific vegetables, consult the individual vegetable sections in Chapter 9.

How much of each crop you grow will be determined by what you like to eat. These crops can be planted in short rows, so a single frame could feasibly grow all of them. How much total frame space you need depends on how much fresh green food you plan to eat. On average, I suggest 2 cold frames (of the 4-by-8-foot size) for each family member to provide fresh food all winter. The consumption of these crops during the fall will open up space for succession plantings of mâche, spinach, arugula, and mizuna.

TABLE 5

CROPS FOR FALL AND WINTER CONSUMPTION

Crop	Planting Dates	Harvest Dates
Arugula	8/1–8/21	10/1–spring
Endive	7/10–7/20	9/15–11/30
Escarole	7/10–7/20	9/15–11/30
Italian dandelion	8/1–8/15	10/1–spring
Lettuce	7/21–9/7	9/15–11/30
Mizuna	8/1–8/15	9/15–11/30
Parsley	6/1–7/15	10/1–spring
Radish	9/1–10/15	10/1–11/30
Scallion	7/1–7/15	10/1–spring
Spinach	8/1–8/30	10/15–11/30
Swiss chard	7/1–8/1	10/1–spring

Second, the frames contain crops for winter and early spring consumption. The later plantings of mâche fill in the spaces left by harvested fall crops. Mâche also can be sown under and between the fall crops and will grow in their shadow until they are harvested. Mâche is the hardiest crop I know. It isn't planted until fall because it germinates best in cool weather. Mâche is your most dependable winter staple for fresh green salads.

TABLE 6

CROPS FOR WINTER AND SPRING CONSUMPTION

Crop	Planting Dates	Harvest Dates
Carrot	8/1	12/1–spring
Claytonia	8/1–9/1	11/1–spring
Italian dandelion	8/1–8/15	10/1–spring
Kohlrabi	8/1–8/15	11/1–spring
Mâche	9/15–11/15	12/1–spring
Parsley	6/1–7/15	10/1–spring
Radicchio	6/1–8/1	12/1–spring
Scallion	7/15–8/1	11/1–spring
Sorrel (perennial)	transplant 9/1	11/1–spring
Spinach	9/15–10/15	12/1–spring
Sugarloaf chicory	7/1–7/15	11/1–spring

Third, the cold frames contain overwintered crops for spring eating. The spinach sowings and the lettuce transplants fill in sections of the frames vacated by crops harvested in the fall.

TABLE 7

OVERWINTERED CROPS

Crop	Planting Dates	Harvest Dates
Dandelion	7/1–7/15	2/15–4/15
Lettuce	9/15–10/15	3/1–5/1
Onion	8/1	4/1–7/1
Spinach	10/1–10/15	2/15–4/15

Most of the crops for winter eating don't do any real growing in the frames during the low sun of midwinter. They grow during the summer and fall, then mark time waiting for spring. That's fine, because the gardener isn't doing much gardening during those months either. The crops in the third category are hibernating. Once the sun returns for longer periods each day (by mid-February at this latitude), you should begin to see the first new growth following the crops' near dormancy in the cold.

Beginning in mid-January, I start sowing short rows of spring crops in any open spots in the frames. These are the succession plantings that will be ready to start picking about the time the winter crops are finished. This group includes arugula, broccoli raab, carrots, claytonia, cress, endive, escarole, lettuce, mâche, mizuna, onions, orach, parsley, peas, purslane, radicchio, radishes, and spinach. In the interests of crop rotation, try to remember what had been growing in that empty spot so as to replace it with a crop from a different family.

COLD FRAME CROP FAMILIES

Amaryllidaceae
Leek
Onion
Scallion

Chenopodiaceae
Beet
Orach
Spinach
Swiss chard

Compositae
Endive
Escarole
Lettuce

Cruciferae
Arugula
Broccoli raab
Cress
Kohlrabi
Mizuna
Radish

Leguminosae
Garden pea
Snap pea

Portulacaceae
Claytonia
Purslane

Umbelliferae
Carrot
Parsley

Valerianaceae
Mâche

Depending on where you live, those tiny spring seedlings and the new growth on the overwintered crops will meet some cold conditions starting in mid-February, when they begin to grow. They will be nipped by frosts and look a little haggard at times before the outdoor temperature begins to rise. Although the sun is out long enough to begin spring in the frames, the outdoor weather is still cold. This is the lag between what I call solar-winter and thermometer-winter. *Solar-winter* is when the sun is at its lowest, the period on either side of the winter solstice that I call the Persephone months. It is determined by the tilt of the earth's axis. It ends by the middle of February. *Thermometer-winter* is the period of the year with the lowest temperatures. It is not synonymous with solar-winter. The coldest temperatures of the year for my garden in Maine usually occur during the first week of February, with a lot of cold still to come.

For me in Zone 5, the 4 weeks from February 15, when the sun starts seriously warming the frames again, to March 15, when the harsh winter cold is over, is the only difficult time in the year-round harvest. Whereas the sun is high enough to start things going, the harsh cold is nipping them back. Even though the cold frame gains extra warmth from the sun during the day, it will still freeze inside when outside nighttime temperatures drop below 25°F. Mâche isn't bothered (I think this wonderfully hardy crop could grow on icebergs), but the variety of other winter crops can be limited in exceptionally cold weather. The farther south you live, the shorter this period will be. You can throw a blanket or insulated cover over the frames at night if you wish, or you can take what nature gives you. Spring is on its way, and by the middle of March, all will be well again.

Watering

For 6 months of the year (October to March), the secret to watering cold frames is to do very little. For 3 of those months (November to January), do none at all. The evaporation of moisture is reduced when the sun is low, and the groundwater table is higher. No water needs to be added. During the transition months, principally April/May and September, you should pay much closer attention to watering because the enhanced warmth inside the frames will increase the plants' need for water compared to the need of outdoor plantings. In summer, the frames are uncovered and will be watered the same as the rest of the garden.

Since I like to water gently, my hose is attached to a watering wand with a very fine rose, which gives a gentle spray. The rose is the plate with small holes at the business end of a wand or watering can. It determines the size of the water droplets. Ideally, a fine rose will ensure that both your watering can and spray wand deliver water as softly as a summer rain.

When you need to apply water to the frames, you can do so by hand or turn on a sprinkler if the frames are open. In either case, it is preferable to water in the morning on a sunny day so the leaves can dry off before evening. When watering by hand, I stand at the lower edge of the frame, open one light, and water the exposed area. Then I put down that light, open the next, and proceed along. If you do not have the experience to judge by garden sense whether you are applying the right amount of water, you can measure and calculate. Use a stopwatch to time how long it takes to fill a gallon jar with your hand sprinkler. Then determine how many square inches are under a light. Knowing that 1 gallon contains 231 cubic inches you can calculate how long it will take to apply ¼ inch, ½ inch, or however much water you want. On average, 1 inch of water per week is recommended, but the quantity of water required will vary with the weather, the season, and the age of the crop.

You might prefer to build an irrigation system for your cold frames. For that you will need a length of PVC pipe fitted with small, 180° spray emitters normally used in commercial greenhouses (see appendix). Attach the pipe to the back wall of the frame, extend one end of the pipe through the side wall, and attach a hose connector. Close off the other end. Then you can

Fig. 34

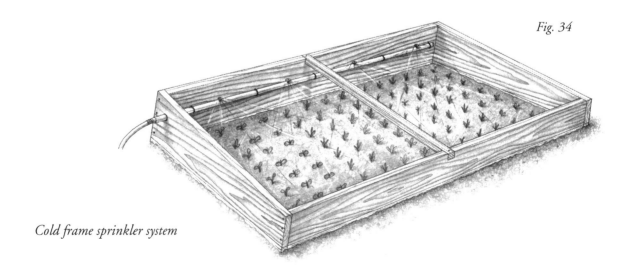

Cold frame sprinkler system

just click the garden hose into the connector to apply water. If you add a simple timer to your system, the water will shut off automatically. The irrigation system should be drained or removed for winter storage to prevent freezing.

If you improve the soil in the frame and add plenty of compost, you will greatly improve the soil's water-holding capacity and structure. This means that the soil can store more water without becoming waterlogged. On a comparison basis, if the water-holding capacity of a volume of sandy soil is 1 unit, an equal volume of clay soil will hold 4 units, but the same volume of soil organic matter will hold 16 units. This is another way in which compost benefits the garden soil.

Direct Sowing versus Transplanting

I transplant the following crops one or more times during the garden year: beets, broccoli, brussels sprouts, cabbage, celeriac, celery, kale, leeks, lettuce, onions, parsley, peppers, and tomatoes. You can direct-seed most of these crops, avoid transplanting, and save yourself some work, but I find there are benefits to transplanting. Some warm-weather crops, such as tomatoes, peppers, and cucumbers, need the head start to produce well in my climate. Some crops, such as celeriac, onions, and leeks, I grow as transplants to give them as long as possible to produce greater harvests. Others, such as the cabbage family, make it through the first weeks after germination with fewer problems when growing in the extra fertility of potting soil. I transplant lettuce for overwintering because I can put the seedlings in after earlier crops have been harvested. In that way, transplanting makes small gardens larger, since other crops can continue to grow in the space that the transplant won't need to occupy for 3 to 4 weeks after seeding. Finally, transplanting is a great way to stay ahead of the weeds. When seeds are planted in the garden, weeds can germinate along with them. Transplants have the advantage of a 3- to 4-week head start.

Starting Plants

My cold frame serves as a greenhouse for starting seedlings. I use it for all seedlings that are transplanted except the early-spring sowings of heat lovers such as tomatoes, peppers, and cucumbers. I start them in a sunny window in the house. For all the others, the cold frame is an ideal place to start growing. Once you begin raising seedlings in the cold frame, you will find it so simple and successful that you will never go back to flats on windowsills. Here's how I do it:

I spread potting mix about 2 to 3 inches deep in whatever part of a frame I wish to use for seedlings. I lay 3-inch boards around the edge as a border, then treat that area as if it were a flat: I make furrows, drop in evenly spaced seeds, cover them shallowly, mark them with name and date on a small stick, and water them lightly with a fine sprinkler. The rows can be as close together as they would be in a flat. I space seeds evenly in the seeding row so they won't be crowded. I try to avoid plant stress at all stages of growing. It takes a little more time, but the results are worth it.

Fig. 35

Cutting the seedlings into 3-inch blocks inside the cold frame

When the seedlings are up, I move them to an adjoining section of the frame, which also has a 2-inch covering of potting mix over the soil. I do this as soon as I can handle the seedlings. Within reason, the younger you transplant a seedling, the better. Dig under each one with a small, pointed dowel, lifting and loosening the roots as you extract them from the soil. Always be gentle with seedlings. Hold them by the leaves, not the stem, so you don't crush the vital parts if you squeeze too hard.

I poke holes in the potting soil of the adjoining section with

Fig. 36

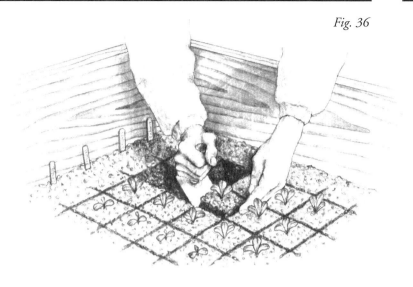

*Scooping up
the seedling with the
transplanting tool*

the dowel to make space for the roots, then tuck them in lightly. I space all seedlings 3 inches apart. When they are large enough to transplant to the garden, I use a knife to cut the soil into 3-inch cubes with a seedling in the center of each. It is just like cutting a tray of brownies. If you make sure the soil is moist (sprinkle if necessary before cutting), the blocks will hold together nicely. Then I use a bricklayer's or right-angle trowel to slice underneath each cube, lift it out, and set it in a tray for transport to its permanent garden home.

Fig. 37

*Planting seedling into the
garden*

I make my own potting soil. The key ingredient is my own 1- to 2-year-old best-quality compost. The other ingredients vary. For example, I might start with a store-bought peat-lite mix (a combination of peat moss and either perlite or vermiculite) and fortify it by adding compost and organic fertilizers. The fertilizers I use are phosphate rock and greensand (see Chapter 2) plus some blood meal as a source of nitrogen. (You can purchase blood meal at the local garden supply store.) I mix all 3 fertilizers together in equal parts to create my special blend. When making mixes, I measure out the bulk ingredients with an 8-quart bucket and the fertilizer blend with a 1-cup measure. A sample formula goes like this:

POTTING SOIL RECIPE I

4 buckets commercial peat-lite mix
2 cups fertilizer blend
3 buckets compost
Mix all together thoroughly.

I usually dump the buckets of ingredients into a wheelbarrow and mix them with a short-handled shovel.

If you want to make a natural potting soil free of any additives that may be included in the commercial peat-lite mix, you can make it as follows:

POTTING SOIL RECIPE II

3 buckets peat moss
2 cups fertilizer blend
1 bucket perlite
3 buckets compost
Mix all together thoroughly.

This formula produces as good a mix as I have ever used. It doesn't need to be sterilized because the compost protects against soil-borne diseases.

Sift any peat moss, compost, or soil for these mixes through a ½-inch screen to remove lumps or stones. When buying peat moss, ask for the best quality available. Some low-grade brands are very dusty and offer little of the air- and water-holding structure that makes peat moss valuable in a mix. If you can't find acceptable peat moss, buy one of the commercial mixes and use the first formula.

Make your potting mix in the fall. All the ingredients will be readily available and not frozen solid, as in late winter. There also appears to be a real benefit to allowing the mix to mellow over the winter. I place my mix in covered garbage cans and store them in the cellar so they won't freeze. Then I'm ready to go as early in the spring as I care to plant.

There are many advantages to growing seedlings in a cold frame. No flats are necessary. There is no potting soil mess in the house. The seedlings will be hardy because the cold frame is not artificially heated. Any additional hardening off is easily accomplished by opening the lights slightly wider. Finally, watering is much less important, since your seedlings are connected to the earth and they can't dry out as quickly as they can in the limited confines of a flat. Thus, an occasional lapse in watering is not disastrous.

The intermediate transplanting from the seedling row to the 3-by-3-inch spacing makes transplanting seedlings a 2-step process. I think it's worth the effort because the intermediate step has been found to stimulate increased root regrowth, resulting in slightly more vigorous transplants. You can do it as a 1-step process by simply starting out with the 3-by-3-inch configuration and planting 3 seeds in each square. After they emerge, you thin to the best one in each square and proceed as before.

With some crops, I use a Dutch idea called multiplants and sow 4 or more seeds in each square with no intention of thinning them. This allows me to grow transplants in groups rather than as singles. The onion crop will serve as a good example of how I go about it. I sow 5 seeds together. I plan for 4 of the seeds to germinate. When the onion seedlings are large enough to go to the garden, I cut out the blocks as usual and set them out at a spacing of 10 by 12 inches. If I were growing single plants in rows they would be set 3 inches apart. Four plants in a clump every 12 inches in a row is the same average spacing as 1 plant every 3 inches. Each onion is allowed just as much total garden space, and the yield is the same. The onions growing together push each other aside gently and at harvest time are lying in a series of small circles rather than single rows. If all the seeds germinate and there are 5 onions in each clump, that's no problem.

In addition to onions, I use the multiplant technique for early transplants of beets, broccoli, cabbage, leeks, scallions, and spinach. Not only is this system more efficient because 4 plants can be transplanted as quickly as 1 but it also can be used to control size when desired. A clump of broccoli, for example, will yield 3 or 4 smaller central heads rather 1 large one. For many families, the smaller unit size is more desirable.

TABLE 8

MULTIPLANT SEEDING

Crop	# of Seeds	Plant Spacing	# of Rows per Bed
Beet	4	6"	3
Broccoli	4	24"	1
Cabbage	3	18"	1
Leek	4	12"	3
Onion	5	12"	3
Scallions	10	6"	3
Spinach	4	6"	3

Winter Harvest

In *Love's Labors Lost,* Shakespeare speaks of winter days when "milk come frozen home in pail." There will be plenty of those days for the four-season harvester. To protect your harvest from freezing, I suggest going to the garden with a covered basket or a pail with a lid. You might even include a few dish towels for extra insulation. I learned this the hard way a couple of times when I absentmindedly joined my children sledding or chatted with a passing neighbor after harvesting. The cold quickly penetrated, and my greens "came frozen home in basket."

The hardy winter greens tolerate freezing and thawing as long as they are growing, but if they freeze after being severed from their roots, they don't usually recover. Nor do they thaw without wilting if harvested while they are frozen. Only mâche can be cut while frozen and still make a respectable showing in the salad bowl. You need to wait until the temperature in the cold

TABLE 9
Harvest Season of Cold Frame Crops

From September to May in Zone 5

Crop	Sept	Oct	Nov	Dec	Jan	Feb	Mar	Apr	May
Arugula									
Beet									
Carrot									
Celery									
Chard									
Chicory, green									
Cabbage, Chinese									
Claytonia									
Dandelion									
Endive									
Escarole									
Kale									
Kohlrabi									
Leek									
Lettuce									
Mâche									
Mizuna									
Onion, green									
Parsley									
Radicchio									
Radish									
Sorrel									
Spinach									

frame rises above freezing before you harvest. Fortunately, the frame temperature will increase on most winter days, whether they are sunny or cloudy. Even on the coldest days, the frame will usually reach harvest temperatures from 11 A.M. to 3 P.M.

During the coldest weather, the freezing temperatures will do considerable damage to the outside leaves of crops such as radicchio, sugarloaf, and escarole. In some cases, the radicchio heads will be surrounded by a layer of mushy leaves. Don't let that put you off. If you peel the mush away, a beautiful vegetable is hiding inside. Although the outer leaves of spinach may turn brown, the smaller center leaves remain in great shape through the coldest weather. Harvest spinach leaves by cutting them an inch above the crown, and the plant will regrow when the weather warms again. Whatever the weather, all the hardy winter crops offer something choice to eat.

Coping with Snow

Most of the time, I clear the cold frames of snow so the sunlight can enter. I use a heavy bristle push broom to do the job. You can use a shovel, but after carelessly breaking the glass on a few lights over the years, I've found that I'm safer with a broom. Sometimes I leave the snow on the frame for insulation if the weather report predicts extra-cold temperatures for a few days following a snowfall. The plants don't mind the dark, and with the extra insulation, the frame temperature won't drop as low. When I've been away and not cleared the frames for many weeks, there haven't been any problems. Remember, the plants are not growing, just hibernating. They don't mind some snow.

Cold Frames Redux

I think the basic cold frame is the most dependable, least exploited aid for the four-season harvest. Table 9 gives an overview of the variety of crops and harvest times that can be expected from cold frame-protected crops in Zone 5.

If you follow the suggestions in this chapter and the discussions about each vegetable in Chapter 9, I assure you a winter garden bounty at least as good as this chart. For those of you who would like to go a step further and ensure the quality and quantity of an even wider harvest of winter vegetables, I offer my experience with a second layer of crop protection—the plastic tunnel—in the next chapter.

CHAPTER 6

THE COVERED GARDEN:
TUNNELS

$\mathcal{Y}$ou can take crop protection a step further than the cold frame. Notice that I continue speaking only of protection, not heat input. This is still a low-tech concept. The cold frame puts a low roof over low plants. The next step is a taller roof over the cold frames and the gardener. The easiest way to do that is with a plastic-covered tunnel greenhouse.

When I use the word *greenhouse*, don't get nervous and hide your checkbook. Many people associate greenhouse with expensive additions to country houses or templelike structures on royal estates with large garden staffs. Those are, admittedly, beautiful examples of greenhouses. But the word encompasses far simpler and less expensive options. Any translucent structure into which the gardener can walk is a greenhouse. All you need is a minimal frame supporting a roof that lets in light.

My greenhouse is basically just a translucent tunnel. The structure consists of curved pipes, like large croquet hoops, spaced at 4-foot intervals. They support a sheet of plastic (polyethylene) that attaches to boards along the ground. This single layer of plastic over a lightweight frame makes the second stage of crop protection an easy option. If you thought cold frames alone were effective, wait until you see the results when they are protected by a tunnel.

If you are handy at bending pipe, you can make your own

structure for a hoop greenhouse. Or you can easily purchase the parts. Inexpensive pipe-frame tunnels are available in 12-, 14-, and 17-foot widths and as long as you want. You also can build a simple greenhouse frame using 2-by-4s with gusseted joints or bowed lengths of fiberglass rods (more on those designs later).

The smallest comfortable size for a food-production greenhouse is about 12 by 12 feet, but I recommend 12 by 20 feet as more serviceable and 14 by 20 feet as even better. Those may seem to be large structures, but they won't be once eating fresh produce in winter becomes a habit. You may even be tempted to make a larger tunnel. Mine is 17 by 32 feet. A plastic-tunnel greenhouse is the least expensive covered space available, so if you have more room inside than you need for the winter vegetable garden, it won't go begging. You can fill it with winter flowers, a sandbox, a barbecue, a hot tub, or whatever else you can imagine. Parkinson's Law also applies to greenhouses: the uses expand to fill the space available.

Low-cost tunnel greenhouses work so well that if the public were more familiar with them, I think every gardening family would have one. They are a very flexible form of crop protection, since they can be erected quickly and covered or uncovered easily. They provide a protected environment that can appear at will—protection that did not exist yesterday but is in place today. There are 2 ways of working with this concept: the mobile greenhouse and the instant greenhouse. Since my inspiration comes from the classic mobile greenhouses of Europe, I'll describe them first.

The Classic Mobile Greenhouse

A mobile greenhouse can be moved from one site to another. Commercial horticulturists in Europe have used mobile greenhouses for over a century. They allow the growers to get maximum use from their financial investment in a greenhouse. The houses sit on railroad wheels and roll on iron rails. The rails extend 2, 3, or more times the length of the house, so many sites are available. A sample cropping sequence might go something like this: An early crop of lettuce is started in the greenhouse on Site 1. When the spring climate is warm enough for the lettuce to finish its growth out-of-doors, the ends are raised and the house is wheeled to Site 2. Early tomato transplants, which need protection at that time of year, are set out in the greenhouse on Site 2. When summer comes and the tomatoes are safe out-of-doors, the house is rolled to Site 3 to provide tropical conditions during the summer for transplants of exotic melons or greenhouse cucumbers.

At the end of the summer, the sequence is reversed. Following the melon and cucumber harvest, the house is returned to Site 2 to protect the tomatoes against fall frosts. Later on, it is moved to Site 1 to cover a late celery crop that was planted after the early lettuce was harvested. Then Site 1 is planted to early lettuce again, and the year begins anew.

Mobile greenhouses have more virtues than just spreading out capital costs. The movable house does not harbor the pest and disease problems that can occur in artificial conditions under cover. There is a similar benefit with cold frames, which are frequently uncovered and moved. The soil benefits from being exposed to the direct effects of the sun, rain, and winter temperatures. These natural forces have a purifying and revitalizing effect on the soil.

Moving frames and greenhouses also allows a more diversified rotation of crops. Although it would be uneconomical to grow a green manure in the expensive confines of a greenhouse, it makes perfect sense to grow one on the uncovered site. Thus, clovers, grasses, and many other crops known to benefit soil health and improve its fertility can become part of the protected crop rotation.

The classic mobile glass greenhouse is quite a piece of work. Although heavy and expensive, it is elegantly and ingeniously constructed. I have copied the inspiration, not the expense. Instead of iron wheels and rails and glass panes, I have wooden skids sliding on wooden rails and a plastic cover. My mobile tunnel is a greatly simplified version and much more manageable than the glass galleons of yore.

Building the Backyard Mobile Tunnel

My mobile tunnel is used year-round. In spring, it gives warm-weather crops such as tomatoes, peppers, and cucumbers a 4-

week head start. In summer, even with the vents and doors open, it provides them with slightly more tropical conditions for enhanced flavor and ripeness. In fall, it extends the summer-crop harvest for a month. In winter, it covers cold frames, providing a second layer of protection for winter vegetables in the frames and a single layer of protection for other hardy crops that are too tall for them.

As we stressed in the previous chapter, however, most of the winter crops are planted during the summer, when the tunnel is filled with heat-loving crops, and most of those summer crops will be started in spring, before the winter crops are finished. How do you deal with that logistical conflict? I move the tunnel. My tunnel has 2 sites—one for summer and the other for winter.

I'm sure you've seen pictures of gardens with raised beds framed by planks. They look more or less the way your cold frames would look if you put soil in them. Well, envision a bed that is 12, or 14, or 17 feet wide—the width of your greenhouse. A row of planks stands above the soil along each edge. The planks are bolted to posts driven into the ground every 4 feet. Those are the rails. The base of my greenhouse, where the hoops attach, is made of planks, as in Figure 38. The 2-by-4-foot skid on the outside edge of the baseboard slides along the top of the rail. I wax the surface to reduce friction.

The forces on the greenhouse hoops tend to push them out at the bottom. Thus, the baseboards run inside the rails, and the natural pressure holds them in tight. The hoops are fastened to the baseboards with bolts and metal plates. A long, straight pipe called a purlin connects the hoops along the top center. That is sufficient structure for most small hoop houses. You can easily adapt a home-built greenhouse made with wooden framing to this system by incorporating the baseboards into the lower structure when you build it.

When you simplify a technology as I have done, you need to think it through thoroughly to prevent problems before they occur. If I can move this greenhouse, so can the wind. It is almost an axiom that if the wind can blow something about, it will. The vision of an object the size of a small house wafting toward me on a stiff breeze is unnerving. Thus, although my mobile greenhouse is simple, it is not casual. When the house is in place, I take precautions to make sure it will stay there. I put ¾-inch-diameter bolts through both the baseboard and the rail every 4 feet and tighten them securely.

Building the Ends

The metal hoops of a tunnel are called *bows*. The end bows need to have a wooden frame bolted to them to allow the plastic cover to be attached. If you purchase a tunnel, you can order framed end bows as an option. Whether you make your own tunnel or purchase one, however, you will want to construct your own end walls. When tunnels are erected conventionally, the end walls are usually built with conventional doors. For the mobile tunnel, you have to do things differently. You need to be able to lift or remove the bottom of each end so as to clear any crops or structures over which the tunnel will be moving.

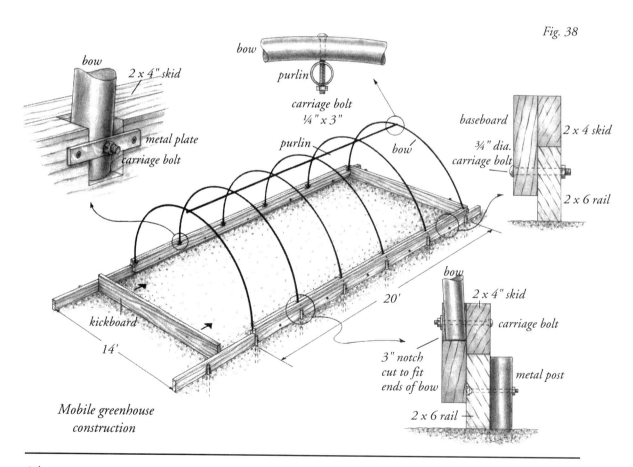

Fig. 38

bow
2 x 4" skid
metal plate
carriage bolt

bow
purlin
carriage bolt ¼" x 3"
purlin
bow

baseboard
¾" dia. carriage bolt
2 x 4 skid
2 x 6 rail

20'
14'
kickboard

bow
2 x 4" skid
carriage bolt
3" notch cut to fit ends of bow
metal post
2 x 6 rail

Mobile greenhouse construction

As the first step in constructing the ends, I bolt a 2-by-4 crossbar horizontally to the wooden frame at each side of the end bow. On most small tunnels, that crossbar will be about 5 to 5½ feet above ground level. I like to leave at least 16 inches between the top of the crossbar and the top of the tunnel arch. I then build 2 doors (see Fig. 39). The lower door is hinged to swing below the horizontal 2-by-4. You can lift it up to open it. A small, conventionally opening door with hinges on the side can be incorporated as part of the structure of a large end door to make frequent entry easier. You will have to duck your head when entering in either case.

Fig. 39

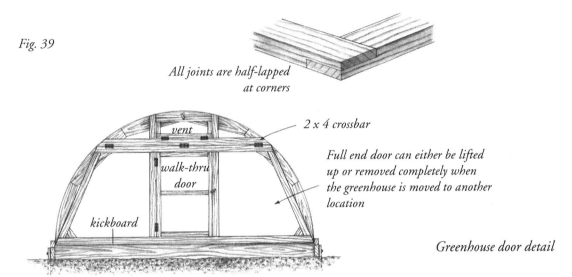

All joints are half-lapped at corners

vent

2 x 4 crossbar

Full end door can either be lifted up or removed completely when the greenhouse is moved to another location

walk-thru door

kickboard

Greenhouse door detail

The upper door, which is also hinged to the crossbar, serves as a vent. I equip this door with an automatic temperature-activated opening arm so warm air will be vented from the tunnel when the inside temperature rises above the thermostat setting. When more venting is needed, the lower doors are either propped open or, as in summer, taken off altogether. I use loose pin hinges so both doors can be removed easily as required.

Door Details

Build the doors carefully to fit the framed end spaces. I construct them out of 2-by-4s, with lapped corners and joints. I use plywood gussets or metal braces at all points of stress. I cover my doors with a single layer of plastic attached on the outward-facing side.

The bottom doors hang to within 10 inches of the ground. A 2-by-12-inch plank extends across the bottom of the opening and is bolted to the bow frames on either side. This plank serves as a kickboard and as the sill for the door to close against at the bottom. By keeping the door 10 inches above the ground, you can make sure that it will clear snow or ice easily when opened in winter. This plank is removed along with the door before the tunnel is moved to a new location.

Putting on the Plastic

The final step is to cover the tunnel. I recommend using a polyethylene plastic made for greenhouses. These products are protected against the degradation caused by sunlight and will last for 3 years. They are available from greenhouse suppliers (check your Yellow Pages).

Choose a calm day to put on the plastic, as wind will make this job very difficult. The technique is to roll out the plastic along the ground on one side of the tunnel and pull one edge of it over to the other side. To make that easier, wrap the edge of the plastic around a golf or tennis ball and tie a rope to the base of that knob. You won't harm the plastic, and you can throw the rope over the tunnel and use it to pull the plastic sheet. A soft broom is useful to push the edge past obstructions. A helper standing on a stepladder under the center of the tunnel can assist the process.

Pull the plastic taut and attach it to the planks at the bottom and sides with two strips of wood. Tack one strip down to hold the plastic and the other to lock it in place (see Fig. 41).

Even if you tighten the plastic when you attach it, there may be times when you wish it were tighter. You can make that process automatic by running a length of soft rope over the plastic-covered tunnel and tying the end to a piece of stretch cord so it is under tension. This tensioned rope (you can use more than one if necessary) will take up any slack that appears in the cover when it expands in warm weather and will not inhibit its contraction when cool weather returns. A tight cover will last longer because it won't be worn by flapping in the wind.

Fig. 40

Using a broom to feed plastic over the top of the frame

The Mobile Greenhouse in Action

The site for the mobile tunnel should be next to or part of the outdoor garden. Since the tunnel site adds year-round growing space, the uncovered garden can be made smaller. The cold frames should be moved to the tunnel area, where they can be doubly protected. I still keep a few frames in the outdoor garden, since that gives me wider climatic options, from the most protected (frames under the tunnel), to the next most protected (the garden frames), to the least protected (the open garden). For example, as the weather gets colder, the fall lettuce harvest will move from the open garden, to the garden frame, and finally to the tunnel-covered frame. In the spring, a wintered-over crop such as spinach will yield first in the tunnel-covered frame, next in the garden frame, and finally in the open garden. The amount of protection is another factor to be used in extending the harvest of a specific crop.

Let's talk about the management of this magic cover. A mobile tunnel that is 14 feet wide by 20 feet long will serve as our example. The rails run east to west, so one of the curved sides of the tunnel faces south for maximum light input. I suggest building the rails twice as long as the tunnel. That means there are 2 potential sites, A and B. How do you manage this operation to make full use of the covered space? Let's begin in a hypothetical fall.

At the moment, the tunnel is on Site A, where it has been all summer. Growing under the tunnel are tomatoes, cucumbers, melons, peppers, and celery. The doors and the vents have been wide open all summer. When the cooler evening temperatures of autumn appear, you begin closing the doors at night. The tender crops are thus protected against the early-fall frosts.

Site B looks like an outdoor garden—which it is, at the moment. There are two parallel 48-inch-wide cold frame beds and one 30-inch standard bed along the south edge. They are separated by 18-inch paths. The standard bed could be growing broccoli, brussels sprouts, leeks, Swiss chard, fall celery, or kale—crops that are too tall for the cold frames. The cold frame beds contain lettuce, spinach, arugula, parsley, scallions, Swiss chard, carrots, mâche, claytonia, radicchio, sugarloaf chicory and a

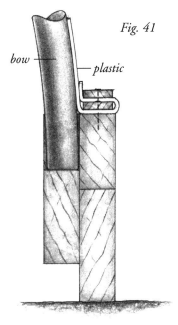

Fig. 41

bow

plastic

Locking the lower edge of plastic to the tunnel frame

TABLE 10
Crop Plan for Mobile Greenhouse

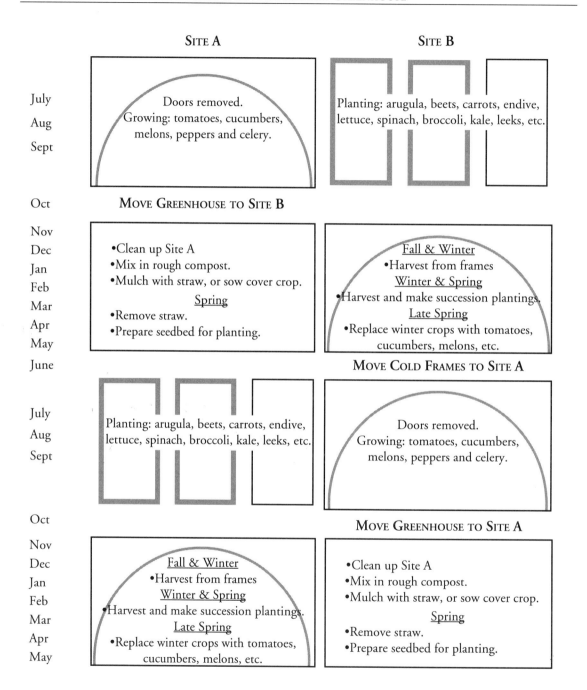

SITE A

SITE B

July
Aug
Sept

Doors removed.
Growing: tomatoes, cucumbers, melons, peppers and celery.

Planting: arugula, beets, carrots, endive, lettuce, spinach, broccoli, kale, leeks, etc.

Oct

MOVE GREENHOUSE TO SITE B

Nov
Dec
Jan
Feb
Mar
Apr
May

•Clean up Site A
•Mix in rough compost.
•Mulch with straw, or sow cover crop.
Spring
•Remove straw.
•Prepare seedbed for planting.

Fall & Winter
•Harvest from frames
Winter & Spring
•Harvest and make succession plantings.
Late Spring
•Replace winter crops with tomatoes, cucumbers, melons, etc.

June

MOVE COLD FRAMES TO SITE A

July
Aug
Sept

Planting: arugula, beets, carrots, endive, lettuce, spinach, broccoli, kale, leeks, etc.

Doors removed.
Growing: tomatoes, cucumbers, melons, peppers and celery.

Oct

MOVE GREENHOUSE TO SITE A

Nov
Dec
Jan
Feb
Mar
Apr
May

Fall & Winter
•Harvest from frames
Winter & Spring
•Harvest and make succession plantings.
Late Spring
•Replace winter crops with tomatoes, cucumbers, melons, etc.

•Clean up Site A
•Mix in rough compost.
•Mulch with straw, or sow cover crop.
Spring
•Remove straw.
•Prepare seedbed for planting.

number of other chicories. All these crops were planted during the summer or are being put in from seeds or transplants as the fall progresses.

Sometime between October 1 and 15 in Zone 5, it is time to say good-bye to the warm-season production. By then, the crops that summered under the tunnel have had their day. Harvest anything that is ripe or will ripen and add the spent plants to the compost heap. Then remove the end door and the kickboard, invite some friends to help push, and slide the tunnel to Site B. It will spend the winter there and protect both the standard bed and the cold frame beds. Since it is too late to sow a green manure crop on Site A, cover the soil with straw or rough compost to protect it over the winter (see Table 10).

For the standard bed on Site B, the single layer of plastic that has just arrived enables you to protect a wider variety of winter crops. Rather than build tall cold frames for broccoli, brussels sprouts, leeks, Swiss chard, fall celery, and kale, you can grow them in the standard bed that will be covered by the mobile greenhouse. Even celery, the least hardy of those mentioned, can be carried in reasonably good shape until the end of November (in Zone 5) under a single layer of plastic. For the winter harvester, the tunnel provides another bonus: not only are the plants more comfortable, but so are you.

The plastic roof over the glass-covered cold frames puts them in another world. The double-covered climate is milder, and the temperature extremes are reduced. All the benefits that applied to cold frames in the open also apply to frames under cover, only more so. This is similar to the envelope house concept in architecture—one building inside another. The inside building, the cold frame, rather than being exposed to the cold of the outside world, is exposed only to the modified temperature within the tunnel—enough of a difference so that the soil will rarely freeze. As a rough estimate, each layer of covering is the equivalent of moving your plants a zone and a half to the south. Thus, for me in Zone 5, a cold frame moderates the temperature to that of Zone 6 plus, and a frame inside a tunnel has its climate moderated to that of Zone 8.

When the outdoor temperature drops to 0°F, the temperature in a standard cold frame will drop to 10° to 20°F depending on a number of factors, such as how warm it was the day before, how quickly the temperature dropped, and how long it stays cold. Under the same conditions, the temperature in the tunnel-covered frame would drop to a range of 20° to 35°F. Actual temperature records from my garden demonstrate these differences (see Table 11). All Figures are in degrees Fahrenheit.

TABLE 11

Temperature Gradients With Protective Structures

Sample nighttime low temperatures			
Outside	Cold Frame	Tunnel	Frame inside Tunnel
-10	6	4	18
0	14	11	25
18	28	24	36

Sample daytime high temperatures (unvented)			
Outside	Cold Frame	Tunnel	Frame inside Tunnel
Sunny day			
5	60	42	78
20	75	60	85
Cloudy day			
30	45	45	60

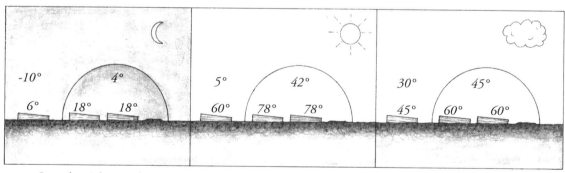

Sample nighttime low temperatures

Sample daytime high temperatures (unvented)

Cloudy day

Notice that the outdoor cold frame is warmer than the tunnel. That is not surprising, since the cold frame is closer to the ground and its glass cover is superior to plastic for retaining soil heat at night. Thus, the tall winter crops growing in the standard beds under the tunnel will not be as protected as they would be under glass. In really cold climates, these crops will benefit from a second layer of protection. In that case, you might want to construct taller cold frames or make small plastic tunnels supported by heavy wire hoops to cover those beds. Or if you have extra lights, you can set them up tepee style to provide taller glass protection. I haven't done either. The nonframe crops under the tunnel do get pummeled by the cold occasionally, but they seem to survive adequately nonetheless.

Layering could go on and on, with third and fourth layers, but just as too many layers of clothing can make you feel awkward, too many layers of glass or plastic inhibit plant well-being by restricting light. Each layer cuts out an additional percentage of light (about 10 to 12 percent minimally and more if the surface is dirty). Two layers are sufficient for the extra climate modification I wish to achieve, and they still let in plenty of light for the plants.

There is one last layer to consider. Some sort of insulation could be rolled over the glass frames at night to provide extra frost protection. Straw mats were used extensively for this purpose by the traditional cold frame market gardeners in years past, and foam blankets are used today. These blankets do increase nighttime protection, but I don't bother with them for a couple of reasons. The first is effort. My system is successful because there is practically no care involved during the winter. All I do is harvest. Remembering to roll out and remove covers would seem like work after a while. I prefer to keep it simple. The second reason I don't use blankets is reality. The old commercial growers used mats because they did not want any small frost nips to mar the sales potential of their produce. But as I noted in Chapter 1, this is my garden and commercial rules don't apply. I don't mind peeling away a little frost damage. I gladly accept minor imperfections in return for freedom from placing and removing insulation twice a day.

Mobile Greenhouse Potential

How far can you go with this mobile greenhouse idea? I have always imagined pampering my palate by extending the system to include three of my favorite foods—asparagus, strawberries, and raspberries. If I were to do that, it might go something like this.

I extend the rails 5 times the length of the greenhouse. Now there are 5 sites—I, II, III, IV, and V. I will grow the following crops on those sites:

I.   Asparagus
II. Strawberries
III. Summer crops
IV. Fall raspberries
V.   Winter crops

Sites III and V are used for basically the same sequence as was described for Sites A and B in the previous section. Sites I, II, and IV are used for growing my favorite foods.

Let's start on March 21, when the tunnel is moved to Site I. Normally in this climate, the first asparagus doesn't appear until mid-May. With the aid of the earlier soil warmth under the tunnel, I can speed that up by 3 weeks. Thus, by late April, I'm ready to move the tunnel to Site II. (Granted, I may lose a few spears to May frosts, but that's a small price to pay.)

Without any protection, the earliest strawberries don't mature here until late June. With the aid of the tunnel to warm things up, I'm looking at a 2-week head start at least.

The next move in this imaginary sequence comes at the end of May when I move the tunnel off the strawberries and onto Site III, where it will spend the summer. There I will be growing warm-season crops as on Site A in the previous sequence.

Everbearing raspberries are growing on Site IV. I move the tunnel off the summer crops on September 21, slightly earlier than under the sequence for Sites A and B. I do it to protect the raspberries against fall frosts. This gives me on average another 6 weeks of raspberries, not to mention a much higher quality of fruit because of the improved growing conditions under the tunnel. When the raspberries are finished in early November, I cut the canes to the ground and add a mulch of compost covered with chipped brush trimmings. The raspberries are then ready for the new season to come.

In the final move of the year, the tunnel goes to Site V, where it spends the winter covering cold frames and standard beds as on Site B in the previous discussion. Next March 21, when the frame crops no longer need the extra protection, the tunnel will return to the asparagus to start the sequence all over again. Gardeners in warmer climates will want to adjust the dates mentioned here to accommodate the times and temperatures in their area.

This is only one sequence. The sites could be growing spring flowers (earlier daffodils and tulips) or fall flowers (mums and calendulas until Thanksgiving). You might move the tunnel to protect a bed of globe artichokes or a group of fig trees in a climate where they would otherwise not survive the winter. Once you turn your imagination loose with this simple harvest extender/ climate moderator, the potential is as wide as your gardening interests.

Modifications for Warmer Climates or Smaller Gardens

A mobile greenhouse allows the gardener to use the same structure in both summer and winter. In climates where summers are warm and long enough that even tender crops don't need greenhouse help, or in gardens too small for two greenhouse sites, another option is available: the instant greenhouse.

Plastic-covered tunnel greenhouses have a minimal structural frame. Consequently, they are diaphanous enough to be unobtrusive if uncovered during the warm months of the year. Thus, you can get part of the benefit of a mobile greenhouse— instant availability—by erecting a permanent greenhouse and covering it only during the cold months. The frame for this permanent greenhouse can be constructed of wood, bowed metal hoops, or any other material that works. The end walls, which we rigged with special doors for the mobile model, would be built with conventional people-sized doors but with an artistic touch. Since the end walls would be basically freestanding during the months when the greenhouse is uncovered, you will want to design them as a visual asset to your garden.

Let's build a greenhouse like this as an example. The dimensions will be the same as for the mobile model: 14 feet wide by 20 feet long. As before, the greenhouse will require 2 end bows and 4 regular bows if they are set at 4 feet apart. Since this tunnel doesn't move, the bows will be anchored by inserting them into lengths of pipe driven into the ground. A board connecting the bases of all the bows along each side provides a surface to which you attach the plastic sheet. I suggest constructing the end walls as in Figure 43. You can paint them or let them weather naturally, as you prefer.

The doors and air vents are removable for the summer. They are designed so that without them, the end walls look like attractive garden arches. The greenhouse structure, without its plastic covering, will look a lot like an arbor. During the summer, runner beans or flowering vines can climb the arches, and trellised crops can be grown up the end walls.

Fig. 43

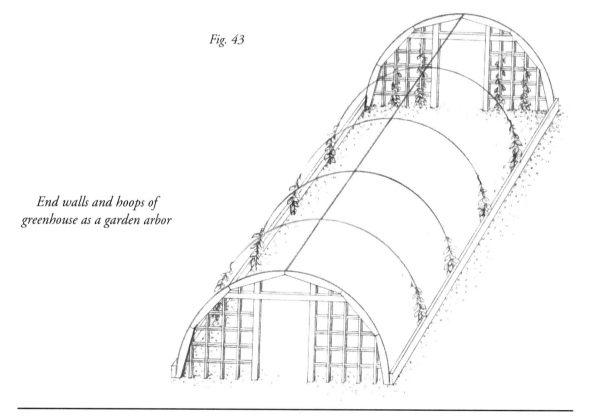

End walls and hoops of greenhouse as a garden arbor

Don't get so enthusiastic with your arbor plantings that you create too much shade. The idea is to be able to plant crops for winter harvest during the summer in the uncovered structure. (See Table 14 for planting dates.) Then when winter arrives, the doors and vents are hung, the ends and the top are covered with plastic, and the next season is under way. Whether this greenhouse will cover cold frame beds so as to give you double coverage or will be the only layer of protection for your winter harvest depends on where you live. Gardeners in Zone 7 and south will find that the greenhouse alone provides adequate protection. Conversely, for much less expense, cold frames alone may be all that is needed.

Temporary Tunnel Frames

You can have an instant greenhouse without a permanent structure. You can make temporary tunnel frames (easy up, easy down) from any number of materials, such as rebar (metal-reinforcing rod), rigid PVC pipe, fiberglass rods, or even saplings. My preference is to make the frame from fiberglass rods that are 20 feet long and ½ inch in diameter (see appendix). You can use these rods to make a tunnel 12 feet wide and 6 feet high in the center. You can make a tunnel that is 20 feet long by 12 feet wide as follows. Lay out two parallel lines 12 feet apart. Make marks every 4 feet (every 2 feet in heavy snow country) along the lines. Insert the end of a rod into the soil (about 12 inches deep) at the first mark, bend the rod over, and insert the other end at the corresponding mark 12 feet away. Continue the process until all the bows have been erected. A 20-foot-long tunnel with bows at 4-foot intervals will require 6 rods.

Take one more rod and tie it to the apex of all the bows as a ridge purlin. One of the best tying materials is a strip of rubber cut from an old inner tube. You can make a very neat job of this by using a couple of I-inch plastic T-joints from the plumbing section of your hardware store. Slip a joint onto each end bow and insert the end of your ridge purlin into the stem of the T.

You can cover this tunnel with 20-foot-wide, 6-mil builder's plastic from the lumberyard. This is the least expensive plastic available. Since it does not contain ultraviolet (UV) inhibitors to protect it against the sun, you will have to replace it every year.

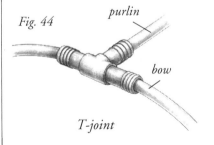

Fig. 44

purlin

bow

T-joint

Instead of attaching the plastic to boards along the ground, this model uses even more basic technology. Dig a little trench along the bottom edge on each side and bury the edges of the plastic with soil. Pack the soil with your feet, and the plastic will be held securely in place. Once the ground freezes, it will not budge.

The end walls for this instant tunnel are made to fit inside the curve of the bow. They are lightweight and prefabricated so they can be put up, taken down, and stored as easily as the rods. They consist of a wooden frame containing a door with a space above it for the automatic vent. The upper corners of the frame are wired to the end bow where they meet. The bottom corners are attached to stakes driven into the ground. The plastic cover for the tunnel is pulled around the end bows and fastened to the wooden frame. It is buried along the bottom edge the same as on the sides.

Fig. 45

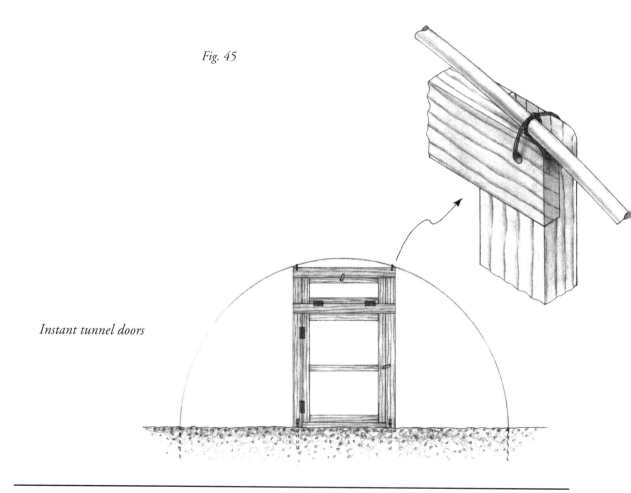

Instant tunnel doors

TABLE 12

HARVEST SEASON OF TUNNEL-COVERED COLD FRAME CROPS

From September to May in Zone 5

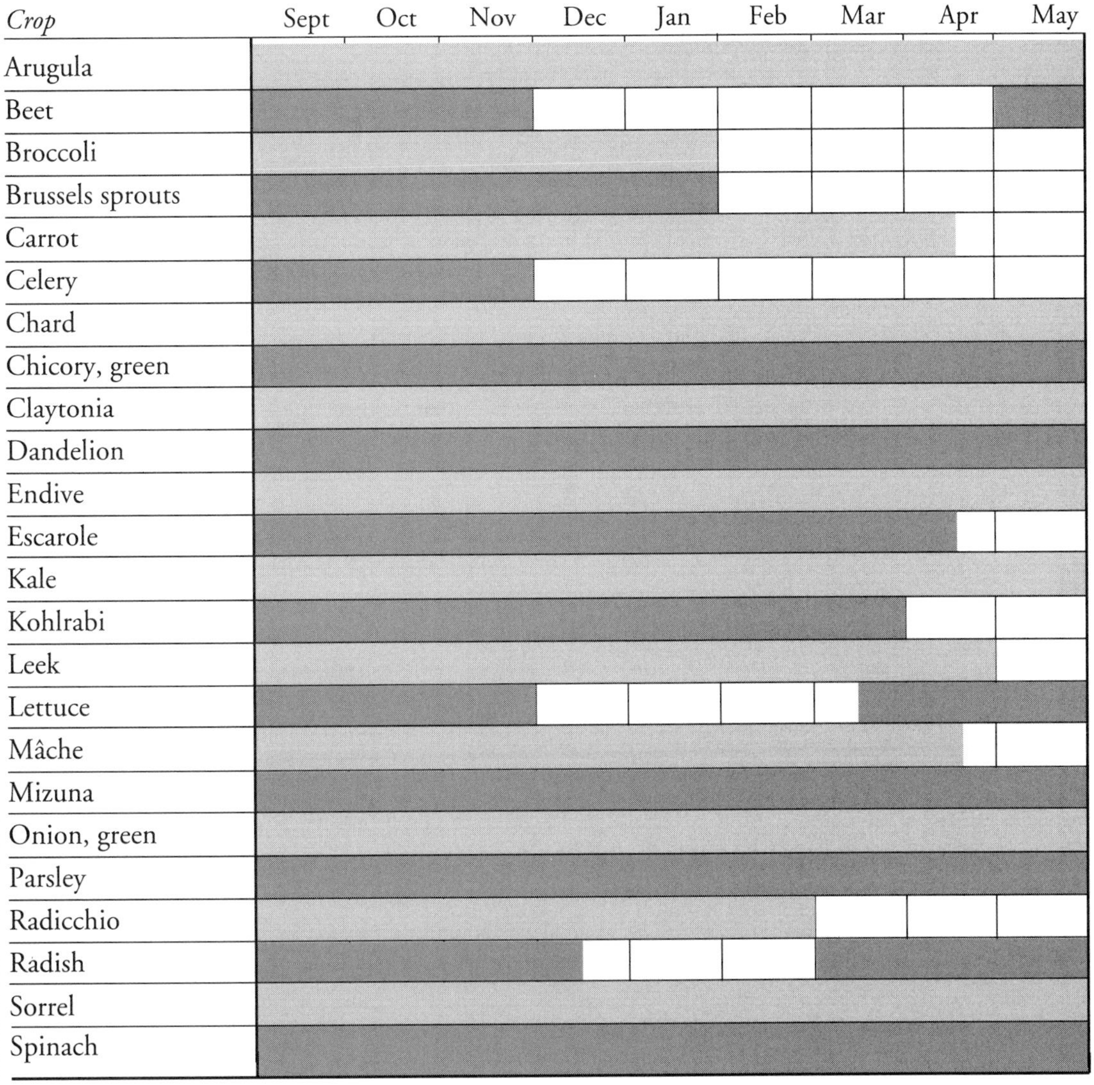
Crop
Sept
Oct
Nov
Dec
Jan
Feb
Mar
Apr
May
Arugula
Beet
Broccoli
Brussels sprouts
Carrot
Celery
Chard
Chicory, green
Claytonia
Dandelion
Endive
Escarole
Kale
Kohlrabi
Leek
Lettuce
Mâche
Mizuna
Onion, green
Parsley
Radicchio
Radish
Sorrel
Spinach

Coping with Snow

Heavy snow accumulation on a tunnel greenhouse can do more than just block sunlight; it can collapse the structure. I don't mean normal snowfalls of 8 to 10 inches, unless the snow is very wet, but the heavy blizzards that come along occasionally. If a big storm is predicted, or if you plan to be away for a while, you should take precautions. Place a 2-by-4 or similar structural upright under the center of every other hoop to provide extra support against heavy loads. Remove these supports when the danger has passed, as they make it awkward to move around in the greenhouse.

Shovel away any snow that slides off the roof. If it's too deep, it not only will block sunlight but also can press in on the side walls of the house and bend the frame. In most years and in most climates, snow will not be a major problem. But you should be aware that on rare occasions it can carry a lot of weight.

The Complete Winter Garden

With the double layer of protection—greenhouse over cold frames—you can harvest a wider range of crops for a longer period of time than under the frames alone. Table 12 gives you some idea of the variety and season of availability of my major winter crops. Table 14 gives planting guidelines far all sections of the United States.

These are not all the known winter crops, but they are the ones with which I have experience. They provide a fabulous winter feast as is, but they will have more company in the future. Keep pushing the possible. There are many other crops for you to discover.

CHAPTER 7

THE UNDERGROUND GARDEN: ROOT CELLARS AND INDOOR HARVESTING

*T*he third simple miracle in this year-round food system is the root cellar—a hole in the ground to store root crops. The root cellar is a basic technology that works in harmony with the natural world, just like compost and cold frames. Whereas compost provides the energy to grow the food and the cold frame provides a winter home for greenery, the root cellar is your winter home for the rest of the garden's bounty.

I think of my root cellar as a secret underground garden into which I spirit away many of my crops when winter threatens. The crops don't grow in this garden. They just sit there respiring quietly and looking beautiful. For them, the most delightful place to spend the winter is not some sunny tropical isle but a cold, damp, dark cavern. If that's what they like, that's what I try to provide. It couldn't be easier.

A root cellar requires no fancy equipment or energy source because it takes advantage of the cold, damp conditions that exist naturally. It will keep working through the deepest winter and the longest power failure. We overlook the miracles it offers because it is so simple and unpretentious. In Zone 6 and north, where winter temperatures dip too low to leave most root crops in the soil or in outdoor pits or buried barrels, the root cellar ensures low-cost cold storage.

The true root crops grow their edible parts underground.

Included in this category are the potato, carrot, beet, radish, and rutabaga, as well as the lesser known celeriac, parsley root, and chicories. For storage purposes, cabbage and kohlrabi are considered root crops because they store well in the same underground conditions. Certain varieties of Chinese cabbage and unrelated crops such as leeks and fall celery also store well for considerable periods.

Creating a Root Cellar

No one wants second best. A slimy cabbage from a dingy corner of the basement will never compete with the crisp specimens on the vegetable shelf of the supermarket. Wilted, dried-out carrots look unappealing next to the crunchy, plastic-wrapped beauties in the refrigerator. When home storage is unsuccessful, a case can be made for artificial refrigeration. But the cabbage need not be slimy nor the carrots wilted. A properly constructed root cellar does not take a backseat to any other method of food storage. It is no great feat to manage a simple underground root cellar so that the produce will be equal or superior in quality to anything stored in an artificially refrigerated unit, even after long periods of storage.

A successful root cellar should be properly located, structurally sound, weather tight, convenient to fill and empty, easy to check on and clean, and secure against rodents. Proper location means underground at a sufficient depth so frost won't penetrate. The cellar should be structurally sound so it won't collapse on you. It needs to be weather tight so cold winds can't blow in and freeze the produce. You need to have easy access to fill it, to use the produce, and to clean it at the end of the winter. And it should be rodent-proof so all the food you have stored won't be nibbled away by rats and mice.

Provision must be made for drainage as with any other cellar, the cellar should be insulated so that it can maintain a low temperature for as long as possible and provide properly humid storage conditions. Finally, microclimates within the cellar (colder near the floor, warmer near the ceiling) should allow you to meet different temperature and moisture requirements for different crops. The cellar will be most successful if it incorporates your underground food-storage needs into one efficient, compact unit. It's surprising how easily a hole in the ground meets all those conditions.

Any house with a basement already has a potential root cellar. You just need to open a vent so cold air can flow in on fall nights and sprinkle water on the floor for moisture. The temperature control in the root cellar is almost automatic because cold air, which is heavier than warm air, will flow down, displacing the warmer air, which rises and exits. This lowers the temperature in the cellar incrementally as fall progresses and the nights get cooler. By the time outdoor conditions are cold enough to require moving root crops to the cellar (around October 21 to November 7 here in Maine), conditions in the underground garden are just right—cool and moist. With minimal attention, they will stay that way until late the next spring.

No wood or other material that might suffer from being wet should be used in root cellar construction. The ideal root cellar is made of concrete or stone with rigid insulation around the outside. Any permanent wood in a root cellar soon becomes damp and moldy. Wood will not only rot but also will serve as a home for bacteria and spoilage organisms and is subject to the gnawing entry of rodents. The stone or concrete cellar is impregnable. It won't rot or decompose, and the thick walls hold the cool of the earth.

The easiest way to make a root cellar is to wall off one corner of the basement as a separate room. The best material is concrete block. There is no problem even if the rest of the basement is heated. You simply need to insulate one temperature zone from the other. Leave enough space between the top of the walls and the joists of the floor above so you can install a cement-board ceiling with rigid insulation above it. Also attach rigid insulation to the heated side of the cellar walls you build. The insulation can be protected with a concretelike covering such as Block Bond. Install an insulated metal door for access, and the structure is complete.

There are several simpler options, especially for storing small quantities of vegetables. If your house has an old-fashioned cellar with a dirt floor and there is enough drainage below floor level, you can dig a pit in the floor 18 to 24 inches deep, line it with concrete blocks, and add an insulated cover. You will want to open the cover every few days to encourage air exchange in the

Fig. 46

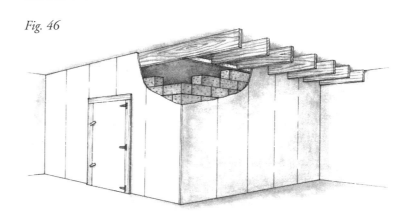

Wall off and insulate a corner of the basement for your root cellar.

Fig. 47a

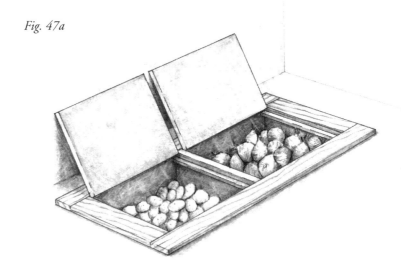

Root cellar option—a buried box works well in cellars with dirt floors.

Fig. 47b

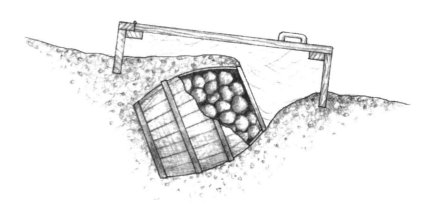

A buried barrel as a simple outdoor root cellar

pit. The pit won't be as easy to use as a room you can walk into, but like any hole in the ground, it should keep root crops cool and moist. In warmer climates, you can use similar pits or buried barrels for storage either outdoors or unheated shed.

Controlling the Temperature

An underground cellar takes advantage of the cool temperatures of the earth. The venting system takes advantage of the cold fall nights to drop the temperature in the root cellar more quickly than it would normally drop. There should be at least one window in the corner of the basement chosen for the root cellar. If there is no window, you will need to provide some opening for air access to the outside. The idea is to establish a good storage temperature before the season requires you to harvest your root crops and put them in the cellar. There is a time lag, since the cellar won't get to the ideal low temperature until late in the fall, but things always work out. Keep the vents mostly closed during the winter. If you let too much cold midwinter air into the cellar, the temperature could drop too low and freeze your crops, although most root crops will not be damaged by freezing unless the temperature goes below 28°F.

The air vent for a home cellar should be at least 12 inches wide by 6 to 8 inches high for adequate airflow. The minimum size would be 6 by 6 inches. It should be screened with ¼-inch hardware cloth. The opening will allow cool air to enter the root cellar and warm air to exit. That natural air movement is what will cool down the cellar in the fall and allow you to regulate its temperature when necessary. The easiest way to manage that airflow is as follows.

Divide the air vent in half horizontally. On the inside of the cellar, use sections of galvanized metal duct to cover the lower half of the window or vent and extend to the floor. This allows the heavy cold air to enter. On the outside of the cellar, install duct to cover the upper half of the window or vent and extend up along the side of the house a few feet. This will act like a chimney so the lighter warm air can exit. That sets up the natural airflow. In autumn, when outside night temperatures begin to drop, both vents are left open. Once cellar temperatures reach the mid-30s, the vents are closed partially or completely to keep the

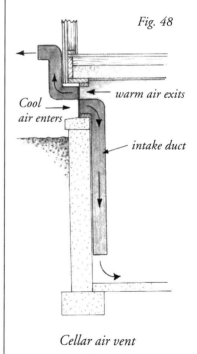

Fig. 48

Cool air enters

warm air exits

intake duct

Cellar air vent

temperature inside the cellar from going below freezing. The ideal temperature for root crop storage is 33° to 36°F. That's the goal, but storage will be adequate even in less than ideal conditions.

To help you keep track of temperature, mount a thermometer in the cellar. Put it near the ground, where the temperature will be the coldest. To take full advantage of temperature levels in a cellar, you can preferentially stack some crops on the floor and others higher up. Beets and kohlrabi like it the coldest. Carrots, rutabagas, radishes, and celeriac prefer the mid-30s. Potatoes do best from 36° to 40°F. Concrete blocks can be used as supports to raise containers above floor level. Storage temperatures for each crop are given in Chapter 9.

After midwinter, close the vents completely to keep the cellar cold as long into the spring as possible. At this time of year, the lag of cellar temperature behind outdoor temperature is just what you want. Of course, the cellar will eventually warm up in summer, but by then everything is fresh from the garden again. Summer is the time to clean out the cellar. Remaining vegetables go to the compost heap. Hose down the walls and ceiling, using a stiff bristle brush to remove any mold. You can apply a coat of whitewash if you wish. A carefully cleaned and managed cellar will store food impeccably.

Controlling the Humidity

In most cases when crops keep poorly and shrivel in cellar storage, the air is too dry. One practice is to store carrots, beets, and others in damp sand, sawdust, or peat to keep them from shriveling. That is a lot of extra work. I prefer to correct the cause rather than treat the symptom. I do that by keeping the humidity high in the storage area.

Roots can be stored directly in boxes or bags with no covering when the cellar atmosphere is humid. I keep the humidity as high as possible (90 to 95 percent) by keeping the floor and walls moist. Whenever I go to the cellar, I take along a bucket of water to splash the walls and floor. I then fill the bucket with food to carry to the kitchen. You may want to mount a humidity meter on the wall along with the thermometer, but the crops themselves are an excellent gauge. If they stay crisp, all is well. If you have to store roots under less than ideal humidity conditions, then packing them in damp sand or sawdust will help them stay crisp.

Keeping the Root Cellar Dark

Any part of the cellar window that is not used for vents should be blocked off completely to insulate and darken the cellar. The best storage takes place in complete darkness. This is most important for potatoes. When potato tubers are exposed to light, their skins turn green and a chemical called solanin is formed. Solanin also is found in potato leaves and is the reason they will give you a bellyache if you eat them. To prevent potatoes from greening in storage, keep them in the dark. The occasional light from opening the door and getting food from the cellar is not a problem. If you have a light bulb in the cellar (which is a good idea so you can see what you are doing), put it on a timer switch. That way it will turn off automatically if anyone forgets and leaves it on.

Storage Containers

Pictures of root cellars usually show wooden bins of root crops and wooden shelves laden with canning jars. My cellar is different. Since I have fresh food year-round in the garden, there's no need for canning jars in my cellar. And, as I mentioned, I avoid wood in cellar construction. I store root crops in bushel-sized plastic

Fig. 49

Root cellar storage containers

boxes that stack one on the other, instead of wooden bins. The woven plastic bags in which grain is sold by feed stores are another option. Five-gallon plastic pails used for bulk peanut butter or yogurt, often available secondhand from health food stores and food co-ops, also work well. Fill them with root crops and stack them on the floor. If you wish to use wooden crates, pay attention to their care. Remove them from the cellar as soon as they are empty. Wash them out, dry them in the sun, and store them dry until next year. They will last much longer and work better that way. The plastic containers also should be cleaned after use. The woven plastic grain bags can be turned inside out and laundered in a washing machine.

Other Stored Crops

For some vegetables, the cold and damp of the root cellar are unsuitable for storage. The onion family and winter squashes keep much better under cool, dry conditions. Both these crops should be allowed to cure in warm, dry temperatures for 2 weeks after harvest. Spread them out in single layers on drying racks in the sun or in the attic. After curing, a mesh bag is the best storage container for onions, and wooden shelves are best for the squashes.

Reasonably ideal winter conditions for storage of these crops can be found in a number of places around the home. Squashes like it warmer (50° to 55°F) than onions (32° to 35°F), so if there are options, let that be your guide. Sometimes the corner of a heated basement farthest from the furnace will suffice. You may have an unheated room in the house or an enclosed porch that doesn't freeze. In many cases, after the weather cools, the attic can provide close to ideal conditions. I have known people who have stored onions and squashes in boxes under the bed in a cool bedroom. Once I stored them under a couch by an exterior wall in the living room, opposite the wood stove. Ingenuity and imagination will help you come up with one solution or another. You will know when you have found the right spot by how long the stored foods keep. Under good conditions, the squashes will last until April and the onions until May.

Check on the condition of your cool, dry vegetables every time you get some for cooking. If the onions start to sprout, you can use the sprouts as you would green onions. If a squash develops mold spots, cut them out and use the rest of the squash within a few days. The more care you took in growing and curing these crops, the better they will hold up in storage.

Really Dry Storage

I use one other storage method—drying. Practically all vegetables can be dried for winter storage, but given the choice, I prefer to eat them fresh from cold frames or the cellar. I have, however, developed one near addiction in this category—dried, vine-ripened tomatoes.

It was when I first dried tomatoes that I finally freed myself of any desire to can vegetables. Tomatoes hung on as the last crop I continued to can because I thought they were indispensable for many of my favorite recipes. They are. But the dried product does it all. What a marvelous food! Dried tomatoes store easily in glass jars and can be used in almost any dish that calls for tomatoes.

If you live in a hot, dry climate, the drying of foods will pose no problem. For those in less favored areas who enjoy a construction project, there are many designs for homemade solar dryers (see appendix). For my dried tomatoes, I have chosen ease and efficiency. I use a small electric air-convection drier with an automatic temperature control (see appendix). It is clean and dependable, and the results are professional. I cut small tomatoes in half and larger ones into 3/8-inch slices, then set them on the drying trays. They are ready in about 12 hours.

I also dry herbs, but I don't need the drier for them. I hang them in bunches from the beams on the kitchen ceiling. They are out of direct sunlight, and the conditions are dry and airy. Their aromas make the kitchen atmosphere that much more delightful. When they feel dry and crinkly, I take them down, separate the leaves from the stems, and store the leaves in opaque glass jars so light won't fade them. The stems go to the compost heap.

Fig. 50

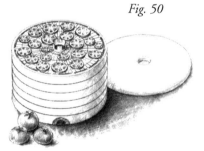

Tomatoes in dryer

The Indoor Garden

The underground garden serves a further culinary function beyond storage of roots to eat during the winter. It is also the source of roots to sprout during the winter. Stored root crops can be coaxed into producing sprouted leaves by moving the roots from the cellar to a warmer environment. This technique is known as *forcing*. The word *forcing* makes the process sound harsher than it is. I prefer to think of it as gentle encouragement.

Stored root crops are biennials. Biennials grow a storage organ (the root) during the first year. They use the food stored in the root to help produce seeds the second year. The leaves that the root grows prior to sending up the seed stalk can be harvested for winter eating. You enable the root to grow those leaves by providing springlike conditions. The expensive Belgian endive, also called witloof or white leaf, that you find in the grocery store is grown that way. You can produce it and many other delicacies as well at home in the winter.

Growing Belgian Endive

The endive you eat (the French call it a *chicon*) is the sprout from a stored endive root. The root was grown in the garden the summer before. Commercial endive growers use special climate-controlled chambers for producing chicons. I find I can do just as well with homegrown conditions. Most important is to find a spot in the house that comes close to the 50° to 55°F temperature for the perfect crop. After that, the rest is easy. I cover the sprouting roots with a black plastic bag to maintain high humidity and keep them in darkness. In my house, a favorite spot is under the kitchen sink.

The temperature emulates spring conditions. In cooler temperatures, the sprout grows more slowly; if the temperature is too warm, it grows too quickly, with some loss of quality. The high humidity keeps the leaves from wilting. The darkness blanches the leaves (keeps them white). Endive is bitter if grown in sunlight. The leaves sprouted in darkness don't contain the bitter quality.

I manage my endive production as follows. When I harvest the roots from the garden in October, I cut off the leaves to within an inch or so of the top of the root. Don't cut it too close, or you will cut off the central bud that grows the largest sprout. I also cut off the bottom of the roots so they are all 6 inches long.

Then I place them, 12 or more depending on size, upright in a 10-quart plastic bucket. I fill around them with sand up to the tops of the roots, then store the buckets in the root cellar.

Starting in late November or early December, when my thoughts turn to winter eating, I bring up 1 bucket every 10 days to initiate the forcing process. (The endive season can last through May, so multiplying 5 months times 3 buckets per month (1 every 10 days) would require storing 15 buckets. When I bring up a bucket, I add water to the sand, place the bucket under the kitchen sink, and cover it with a large black plastic bag. Every few days, I check to make sure the sand is moist and add water if necessary (better too wet than too dry). Within 3 weeks, I'm eating delicious Belgian endive. The parade of new buckets maintains the supply all winter.

Harvest is simple. You cut the chicon off where it meets the root. When all the chicons are harvested, remove the bucket, put the roots on the compost heap and the sand on the icy driveway, and store the bucket till next year. If the chicons begin to grow too large, you can harvest all of them at once and store them in the refrigerator. It's possible to get a second (and third) harvest of smaller chicons from the outer buds on the root, but I prefer to move on to the prime chicons from the next bucket.

If temperatures are too warm or if you grow a variety of Belgian endive that was bred for growing *under* a covering of sand rather than just planted in sand, the leaves on the chicons may open out at the top rather than remaining pointed. That is only a problem for the commercial grower, who wants to sell a perfectly shaped product. The less than perfect chicon will taste just as good chopped in your salad or baked in a cheese sauce. This should not be a problem, though, since the modern varieties of Belgian endive are all bred for uncovered production.

You can use this same forcing process for other members of the chicory family or for close relatives, such as the dandelion. The sprouts may not be classic in shape, but they will taste good. Once you realize how productive this can be, you might want to try forcing some of the less familiar subjects. In addition to those forced in darkness, a number of food crops can be grown in the light. It is a case of sacrificing the root to get it to grow leaves.

Fig. 51

Endives sprouting in buckets of sand

TABLE 13
AVAILABILITY OF ROOT CELLAR CROPS

	Cellar Storage ☐		Cool, Dry Storage ▨		Forced in Warmth (for leaf production) ■			
Crop	Oct	Nov	Dec	Jan	Feb	Mar	Apr	May
Beet	Cellar	Forced	Forced	Forced	Forced	Forced	Forced	Forced
Belgian endive		Forced	Forced	Forced	Forced	Forced	Forced	Forced
Cabbage	Cellar	Cellar/Forced	Cellar/Forced	Cellar/Forced	Cellar/Forced	Cellar/Forced	Cellar/Forced	Cellar/Forced
Cabbage, Chinese	Cellar	Cellar	Cellar	Cellar	Cellar	Cellar		
Carrot		Cellar	Cellar	Cellar	Cellar	Cellar	Cellar	Cellar
Celeriac	Cellar	Cellar/Forced	Cellar/Forced	Cellar/Forced	Cellar/Forced	Cellar/Forced	Cellar/Forced	Cellar/Forced
Garlic	Cool	Cool	Cool	Cool	Cool	Cool	Cool	Cool
Kohlrabi	Cellar	Cellar	Cellar	Cellar	Cellar	Cellar	Cellar	
Onion, bulb	Cool	Cool	Cool	Cool	Cool	Cool	Cool	Cool
Parsley root	Cellar	Cellar/Forced	Cellar/Forced	Cellar/Forced	Cellar/Forced	Cellar/Forced	Cellar/Forced	Cellar/Forced
Potato	Cellar	Cellar	Cellar	Cellar	Cellar	Cellar	Cellar	Cellar
Radish	Cellar	Cellar	Cellar	Cellar	Cellar	Cellar	Cellar	Cellar
Rutabaga	Cellar	Cellar/Forced	Cellar/Forced	Cellar/Forced	Cellar/Forced	Cellar/Forced	Cellar/Forced	Cellar/Forced
Squash, winter	Cool	Cool	Cool	Cool	Cool	Cool	Cool	

Forcing Winter Greenery

From the cellar I bring up celeriac, beets, and parsley root and plant them in large pots of damp sand in a sunny window. You also can do this with turnips, onions, and carrots. There is no need for darkness because, in this case, I want the new growth to be green. I water the pots every few days to keep the sand damp. The room temperature (60° to 65°F) is ideal. The vigor of the roots themselves determines the quantity and quality of your production. You will learn to adjust your harvesting techniques and growth expectations accordingly. The celeriac grows small, flavorful celery stalks; the beets grow beet greens; and the parsley roots produce a pretty good parsley. The turnips grow turnip greens, the onion tops can be used like green onions, and the ferny carrot tops make a nice nibble. Even the smallest shoots of sprouted greens are a flavorful garnish for a midwinter dish.

Fig. 52

Sprouting cabbages

To add bulk to a salad, you may try another winter growing idea from the underground garden. When you harvest cabbages in the fall, remove the loose outer leaves and pull the cabbages—head, stem, and roots—from the soil. Store them upright on the cellar floor, leaning against the wall with a little sand over their roots. They store very well that way. When you bring a cabbage up to the kitchen, cut the head off for eating, then plant the leftover roots and stem in an upright position in one of the damp sand pots in the window. Add water to keep the sand moist. Within a few days, sprouts will begin to grow from the leaf nodes all along the stem. You will soon have a bushy mound of fresh green cabbage shoots, which are the foundation for many a fine winter salad, soup, or casserole.

CHAPTER 8

THE NATURAL GARDEN: PLANTS AND PESTS

y garden exists as a part of the natural world, and I pay attention to the patterns of that world. Thus, I don't speak in terms of secrets to gardening success. There are no secrets. The facts are written on every piece of field and forest right in front of your eyes. The plants that grow best are those whose needs are best met by that soil. The soil consists of varying mixtures of air, water, organic matter, and rock particles. My role as gardener involves modifying those soil factors to establish ideal conditions for vegetable crops. The interconnections between soil nutrients, soil structure, soil organisms, and the health of plants in the garden may appear complex until you see that they follow logical principles. This is not complexity but wholeness; not chaos but elemental order. I have a simple rule: if what I am doing in the garden seems complicated, it is probably wrong.

This approach to gardening celebrates my partnership with nature, but I am definitely the junior partner. The more time I spend in the garden and the more reading and studying I do about gardening, the more impressed I become—awed, actually—by nature's design. There are enough miracles in my garden soil to fill hundreds of books. There are more fascinating creatures and more interconnected activities in the world under my feet than I could ever imagine. These soil activities all function because the soil is a world of fluid and dynamic balances. It is a world of life, growth, death, decay, and rebirth where all the parts of that cycle have their indispensable roles. It is a world where not only the woodchuck but also the maple leaf, the wilted daisy, and the mandrake root vanish to leave behind a poem. It is also a world where there is an answer to pests (insects and diseases) that doesn't involve poisons.

As the reader may have inferred from my fascination with the life processes of compost and fertile soil, I have little use for the fragmentation of natural processes caused by the shortcut of agricultural chemicals. Whether intended as drugs to induce artificial fertility or as weapons to turn live creatures into dead ones, chemicals attempt to influence single parts of a rich and interconnected system. Chemicals miss the elegance. They were conceived in an age of hubris by minds that ignored the marvelous balances of the natural system. They have persevered in an age of awareness through the aggressive marketing of large industrial concerns. The peddlers of chemicals appreciate the sales potential of products that need to be applied frequently and create user dependence by their mode of action.

Although chemical fertilizers may imitate the life processes of the soil, they carry none of the health and vigor of true soil fertility. Chemicals maintain the growth of plants in subfertile soils by supplying a small percentage of the essential nutrients. Chemicals may be defensible as an occasional tool when difficult conditions occur, but as a permanent input, they divert attention from correcting the problem that exists. They treat the *symptom,* poor plant growth, and ignore the *cause,* a lifeless, subfertile soil. The gardener who temporarily stimulates plant growth in a dead soil by using lifeless chemicals ignores the far more effective practice of nurturing the innate productive capacity of the earth by adding an organic compost teeming with life.

Pesticides are similarly misconceived. They are a crude bludgeon. The use of poisons to attack pests ascribes a malevolence to the natural world that is belied by even a quick look at the intricate system of balances that nature maintains. Like chemical fertilizers, pesticides treat the symptoms rather than correct the causes. The symptoms, insects and diseases, are visible indications that all is not well with the plant, just as a headache is a symptom that all is not well with me. My garden has taught me clearly over the years that pests are not enemies;

they are indicators—signals—of plant stress. If I heed the signal, I can act to prevent the cause. The cause of the plant stress is some malfunction in the growing conditions for the plants. Plants under stress are susceptible to pest problems.

Let me state that point again because it is basic to my philosophy of gardening. There is a direct relationship between the growing conditions of plants and the susceptibility of those plants to pests. Problems in the garden are our fault through unsuccessful gardening practices, rather than nature's fault through malicious intent. The way to approach pest problems in the garden is to correct the cause rather than treat the symptom. Not only does correcting the cause solve the problem, but it keeps the problem from recurring so it does not have to be treated again tomorrow and the day after and the day after that. I have come to these conclusions after 25 years of observation and experience in vegetable growing.

I am not alone. There is extensive scientific evidence that negative changes in the internal composition of plants can result from imbalanced fertilization and inadequate growing conditions. Those changes affect the resistance of plants to insects and diseases. When the growing conditions are improved by adding compost, aerating the soil, watering, letting in the sun, and so forth, the symptoms (pests) disappear—just as my headache will go away when its cause (emotional stress, polluted air, allergy-producing food) is removed. If I take a painkiller for the headache, I risk other complications as a consequence. Similarly, if I use pesticides to kill a pest, I risk upsetting other balances in the garden system that may exacerbate pest problems in the future. If, however, I improve the growing conditions that benefit plants, I can tip the balance in the plants' favor without disrupting the system.

How do you learn to correct causes of pest problems in your garden? A good way to start is by imagining yourself as the roots of a plant. Would you like to live in that soil? Is it too compact or too fluffy? Too wet or too dry? Are there enough of both the major and minor nutrients? Will the soil provide all the lesser-known and only slightly understood benefits of a well-decomposed compost? All gardeners instinctively recognize the rich, dark, fertile look of a soil that has been well cared for. That is what the roots of plants will thrive in. That is what you want to create. (The soil fertility information and techniques in Chapters 2 and 3 tell you how.)

Why is it that insects multiply on stressed plants and not on unstressed ones? The best explanation I have found goes something like this. Most insects remain at a low population level in relation to the potential amount of food around them because there is inadequate nitrogen in that food for insect nutrition. When plants are stressed by poor growing conditions, one consequence is that they become a richer source of nitrogen. In other words, stressed plants become an insect snack bar.

How does this process work? The scientific evidence indicates that the effect of stress on a plant—whether from lack of nutrients, excess or deficiency of water, soil compaction, temperature, or other soil or environmental factors—is to inhibit the synthesis of protein by the plant. When protein synthesis is inhibited, the plant accumulates increasing levels of amino acids (free nitrogen) in its aerial parts, especially the phloem. Under nonstressful conditions, those amino acids would have been used by the plant to form protein. As mentioned, insects thrive on plants high in free nitrogen and are thus attracted to and feed upon those plants. When protein synthesis proceeds normally, the nitrogen is locked up in completed protein. The insects are not attracted to unstressed plants because they cannot feed successfully on them.

Farley Mowat describes a similar example of the balance between predator and prey in his story of wolves and caribou in *Never Cry Wolf* (Bantam, 1984). Mowat was expecting to see wolves slaughter caribou indiscriminately. He was puzzled when he saw wolves only scaring the caribou and watching them run. The wolves seemed to be testing the caribou. Mowat's Eskimo companion, Ootek, told him this was precisely what was happening. Wolves cannot catch a healthy caribou. They can catch only the weak, the sick, and the unfit. By testing the caribou to see them run, the wolves hope to spot any that are below par. Ootek explained that there was a balance between the wolves and the caribou. After hard winters, when the caribou are stressed and weakened, the wolves can catch more of them, and the wolves thrive. When the winter is mild and adequate food supplies favor the caribou's well-being, the wolves are at a disadvantage. Ootek understood instinctively that the predator-prey relationship was part of the elegant balance of natural systems.

From my experience, the same situation exists in a well-composted garden. Healthy, unstressed plants are not bothered by insects. Despite the amount of scientific evidence that backs up this theory, the idea meets great resistance. It seems too good to be true. In a wonderful passage in the book *Organic Farming* by Hugh Corley (Faber, 1957), an English organic farmer, Corley pauses at this same stage in his discussion of the idea to say, "Now I quite sympathize with the sceptical reader who up till now has thought me a fairly moderate crank and not as mad as some organic enthusiasts—and who now says, 'Well, really, there are limits to what I can believe!'" (p. 172).

In my many attempts to explain this concept to gardening audiences, I have seen that look of sceptical disbelief often enough. I call it the Brooklyn Bridge look. "And if I believe that, you'll tell me next that you have a bridge in Brooklyn to sell me." Why is this idea so difficult to accept? Is it just because we are unfamiliar with it?

I think there are deeper reasons. We have difficulty understanding a benevolent nature with elegantly simple systems because we have made nature in our own image. As members of the human species, we find ourselves surrounded by conflict, confusion, violence, and war. We interpret nature to fit our pattern. We see natural processes as if they were projections of our actions. Thus, we see malevolence in the relationship of one organism to another and in nature's relationship to us. We don't notice the beneficial balances between predator and prey that are maintained throughout the natural world. We miss the obvious garden logic of tipping that balance in our favor by creating optimum growing conditions for our plants. Instead we see the temporary agents of that balance (insects and diseases) as threatening forces to be battled and defeated. We need to look again.

It can be a refreshing mental exercise to look at something familiar from a different perspective; to reappraise nature as a system that is not malevolent but benevolent; to see "pests" as helpful signals or indicators, not enemies; to see the relationship between predator and prey as natural management rather than violence; to understand that when we work against the system by killing pests and doping up sick soil we are contributing to the problem. We need to reevaluate our place in the garden. The gardener's aim is not to protect sick plants but to enable healthy ones. You enable plants to attain their natural insusceptibility by removing plant stress. You remove plant stress by working to optimize all those factors involved in plant well-being that I have emphasized in this book.

I do not spray my garden, and I have no pest problems to speak of. I can refer you to organic gardeners and farmers all over the world who have the same experience. Occasionally, when I think I have done everything right, the system goes against me. It shows me that I haven't yet achieved adequate growing conditions for that particular crop. The majority of problems usually solve themselves after the first 3 years in a well-composted garden.

A few pest problems may appear occasionally. Sometimes a crop is hard to adapt to my soil or climate. In most of those cases, if I just observe, I find the eventual damage so slight as to be no bother. The more difficult cases I can often solve by changing varieties. Once or twice I have given up on a crop until I Figured out what I was doing wrong. I know some low-impact cures and palliatives for those difficult moments (for example, a vacuum cleaner is very effective against flea beetles, cucumber beetles, potato beetles, and Japanese beetles), and I will mention them on a crop-by-crop basis in Chapter 9. Some of them involve cultural practices; others use physical barriers. There are also a few "safe" pesticides to use only as temporary crutches. I much prefer correcting the cause of the problem. That preference reflects a philosophy that is important not only in the garden but also in the broader world beyond.

We live in a world that has practiced violence for generations—violence to other creatures, violence to the planet, violence to ourselves. Yet in my garden, where I have nurtured a healthy soil-plant community, I see a model of a highly successful, non-violent system where I participate in gentle biological diplomacy rather than war. The garden has more to teach us than just how to grow food.

CHAPTER 9

THE CAST
OF CHARACTERS

Globe artichoke

ARTICHOKE, GLOBE *Cynara scolymus*

Planting Distance—1 row per 30-inch-wide bed; plants 24 inches apart.

Crop Rotation—Related to chicories, dandelion, salsify, and lettuce.

Growing Tips—Rich soil, lots of organic matter, and plenty of moisture. Mulch heavily for best results.

Storage Tips—Can be stored in the refrigerator for 2 weeks.

Variety Tips—For annual culture • *Grande Beurre*

Yes, you can grow globe artichokes in cold climates where they don't survive the winter. I have grown them in the chilly mountains of Vermont and on the cool coast of Maine. Other gardeners have succeeded all around the country. The trick is to turn the artichoke from a biennial into an annual. All that's required is a little horticultural sleight of hand.

If you plant an artichoke seed, it will usually grow only leaves the first year. The following year, it will send up a stalk from which grow the artichokes—actually edible flower buds. If the winter is too severe (as winters in most of the northern half of the United States are), the first-year vegetative plants won't survive to become second-year producing plants. The sleight of hand involves fooling the plants to think they are 2 years old in the first year.

To achieve that, you need to grow the young artichoke plants first in warm and then cool temperatures. Start the seeds indoors in a warm, sunny window 6 weeks before the earliest date on which you could safely move them to a cold frame. Move them to a cold frame when you are sure the temperature inside the frame will no longer go below 25°F. In Vermont, I sowed on February 15 and moved the plants to the frame on April 1. Once they are in the frame, leave the frame open as much as possible. The cooler they are for the next 6 weeks, the better.

The change of growing temperatures from warm to cool is what fools the plants. The first 6 weeks of warm growing conditions were sufficient time for the plants to complete their first "summer" season. The subsequent 6 weeks of cool temperatures make them think they have experienced their first winter. Thus, although they are only 12 weeks old when I transplant them to the garden, they think they are beginning their second year. The second year is when artichoke plants begin to produce the flower buds that we eat as artichokes. And so they do.

The care they receive after transplanting to the garden will determine the number and size of the artichokes. Under the best conditions, I have averaged 8 to 9 artichokes of medium to medium-large size per plant. The best conditions are plenty of organic matter (mix in compost, manure, or peat moss generously) and plenty of moisture (mulch with straw and irrigate regularly).

I space the plants 24 inches apart in a single row down the center of the 30-inch-wide bed. That is much closer spacing than for perennial artichokes, but these plants won't get as large. I harvest by cutting the stem beneath the bud with a sharp knife. Don't wait too long. Once the leaf bracts on the bud begin to open, the flesh gets tougher and more fibrous. Almost any variety of seed-sown artichoke will work to some degree under this system, but there is one exceptional variety that is better adapted than any other—*Grande Beurre* from Thompson & Morgan. *Green Globe,* available from a number of sources, is a second choice. In New England, the production season is August and September—2 months of the best, freshest, and most flavorful artichokes you will ever eat.

ARUGULA   See SALAD GREENS

ASPARAGUS   *Asparagus officinalis*

Planting Distance—1 row per 30-inch wide bed; plants 24 inches apart.
Crop Rotation—None needed; perennial.
Growing Tips—Asparagus will thrive on all the compost and manure you can spare.
Storage Tips—Can be stored in the refrigerator for 1 week.
Variety Tips—For dependability • *Viking*

Asparagus is the classic spring food to anticipate, to enjoy, and to anticipate again. It seems almost magical when asparagus spears begin poking out of the soil just after winter has lost its grip. Either nibbled raw while I harvest or served in one of a dozen different ways, asparagus is my favorite gourmet vegetable.

The asparagus plant is a well-designed system. The roots are a food storehouse and resemble a thick-legged octopus living underneath the ground. The food stored in the roots is what allows the asparagus plant to keep sending up new stems (spears) in the spring despite the fact that the gardener keeps cutting every one of them off. That's why there has to be an end to the harvest season after a month or two. The plant needs to spend the rest of the growing season storing up more food from photosynthesis by its ferny leaves to be able to put up with the same exhausting process again next year.

Logically, the more you can enhance food storage, the more vigorous the production. But asparagus tends to be forgotten as the season progresses. Its virtue, the dependability of coming back every year at a time when fresh vegetables are treasured, is often its downfall. Lavish attention is paid to asparagus in the picking and eating season, and then it becomes just a ferny background. At that point, weeds and inadequate fertility will hamper next year's crop. Asparagus doesn't need to be pampered, but it does need to be weeded, watered, and fed.

The asparagus bed should be weeded at least 2 times. The first weeding is early in the spring. That is necessary because the worst weed in asparagus is asparagus itself. Asparagus plants produce seeds in that ferny growth (except for the new sterile male hybrids). Asparagus seeds sprout into volunteer plants that will crowd the bed and lower the production of quality spears. They are easily controlled. Volunteer asparagus germinates near the soil's surface. Your producing asparagus plants will have their crowns well below the surface. A vigorous, shallow hoeing of the bed in early spring will discourage the interlopers.

The second weeding period comes at the end of the harvest. Make a point of cultivating every so often for the next few weeks to prevent weeds from getting established. Once the stalks get tall and ferny and cast shade, you should have little problem except with perennial weeds. Perennial weeds such as witchgrass can be the death of a perennial crop such as asparagus. Be vigilant and watch for invasion from the edge of the patch. Dig up witchgrass plants and their roots when you see them. Prevention is the key.

Feeding the asparagus bed is best done in the fall. If you want to be lavish with organic matter, this is the crop to pamper. It is hard to overfeed asparagus. I have used compost, manure, and fresh seaweed, all with good results. The fall feeding prepares the bed for vigorous spring growth. Before feeding, cut and remove the asparagus fern. Wait until it has turned brown but before too many of the red berries containing the seeds have fallen. Spread the manure or compost over the surface of the bed and cover it with a few inches of straw for winter protection. Remove the straw in the spring. The early spring hoeing will incorporate the compost or manure residue into the surface soil.

The final ingredient in asparagus care is water. Whenever the rest of the garden needs to be irrigated, I guarantee that the asparagus also will benefit from the extra water. The fern will grow taller and be more vigorous. That vigor will be reflected in next year's harvest.

Asparagus is a perennial and the ferns are tall. People usually recommend establishing the bed in an out-of-the-way location where it will not cast shade. That may be why it's often ignored in the off-season. I think it's wiser to put the bed wherever the sun shines and the soil is fertile. That way you can tuck a few lettuce or spinach plants in its shade during the hotter months of the year.

You can establish an asparagus bed by purchasing crowns or growing your own plants. I prefer the latter. These strong little seedlings fit nicely in a standard 4-inch pot. If you have a greenhouse, you can start them 6 months before the last spring frost and get production a year earlier, but 2 months ahead is fine. I set out the plants in the bottom of an 8-inch-deep hole made with a post-hole digger. I space them 24 inches apart down the center of a standard bed. I fill the hole with enough soil to cover partway up the plant stem. As they grow taller, I continue to add soil until it is level with the bed. I plan to harvest my first asparagus spears 2 years after setting out the seedlings. At harvest, cut the spears just below soil level, being careful not to injure spears yet to emerge. A very sharp, fishtail-shaped asparagus knife is the tool of choice.

Harvesting asparagus

BEAN   *Phaseolus* spp.

Planting Distance—Rows 16 to 18 inches apart across bed; seeds 3 inches apart; thin to 6 inches apart.

Crop Rotation—Beans are a legume and are related to other legumes such as peas and clovers.

Growing Tips—Sow seeds eye down for best germination.

Storage Tips—Can be stored in the refrigerator for a few days, but are much better freshly picked.

Variety Tips—Bush bean • *Triumph de Farcy*
Pole bean • *Fortex*

Beans offer more variety than any other crop. If you include the dry beans, there is sufficient range of color, pattern, size, shape, and flavor to provide a lifetime of gastronomic fascination. I have known seed-saving enthusiasts with collections of hundreds of distinct varieties of dry beans. Among the green beans, you can choose varieties based on length, diameter, color, flavor, and tenderness. The delights of many of the green beans are available only to the home gardener.

A customer at my market stand began a conversation by remarking on the exceptional quality of our green beans. I agreed that they were good, but this gentleman was positively effusive, and with good reason. He was the president of a company that processed gourmet canned and frozen vegetables. He said the crop that most dissatisfied him was green beans. The varieties suitable for machine picking and processing were not the exceptional culinary varieties. They just didn't have the same fresh snap and flavor. He said that he dreamed of the day his company could process beans as good as ours.

He knew his beans. Fresh eating beans are thin and tender and don't all mature at once. They are not pickable by machine. Processing beans need to be tougher and more fibrous to survive picking and processing. Will the two ever meet? Someday, maybe, but for my part I grow only the best eaters, and I enjoy them fresh for as long a season as possible. Although I prefer the thin French *filet* types, others favor a thicker, fleshier bean. Fortunately, there is a wide selection of fresh eating varieties for all tastes.

Green beans need to be picked every day or so for the best quality. They are a perfect crop for the small succession plantings of the four-season garden. If you plant too many beans, you have to pick more than you want or feel guilty because you haven't kept up with them. Not so with small, succession plantings. When there are too many beans, you just yank out the older plantings and add them to the compost heap, then replant to some other crop. The new beans will continue producing until their replacement comes along. Of course, if you grow a variety that develops good-size seeds, you can leave the old plants and harvest them later as shell beans.

I plant beans in short rows across the beds. Since I like to thin green bush beans to at least 6 inches apart, there may be only 5 or 6 plants in a 30-inch row. That's ideal. A few short rows like that in each succession planting will keep the bean harvest well

Plant bean seeds with eyes looking down

managed. I put the rows 16 to 18 inches apart. You may want to modify that spacing depending on the variety of bush bean you prefer. If the plants do get too crowded, cut off and compost every other one.

I plant pole beans in the trellised beds along with other climbing crops. I put 4 seeds in each hill with 16 inches of space between hills. The vines grow up a single length of untreated 4-ply garden twine tied to the trellis at the top and buried in the soil at the bottom. When they are through producing, I cut the twine and compost the vines, twine and all.

BEET   *Beta vulgaris*

Planting Distance—2 or 3 rows per 30-inch-wide bed; seeds 1 inch apart; thin to 2 to 4 inches apart.
Crop Rotation—Related to Swiss chard, spinach, and orach. Beets do well following a leguminous green manure.
Growing Tips—Beets benefit from fertilization with seaweed products.
Storage Tips—Store in root cellar at 32°F. Beets keep better than any other root crop.
Variety Tips—Early • *Red Ace*
　All-around use • *Formanova, Detroit Dark Red*
　Winter storage • *Winter Keeper, Long Season*

Beets are one of my favorite vegetables. I often feel like a proselytizer for *Beta vulgaris*—a red root rooter. I think they are far more delicious and adaptable than their public image might indicate. I have been told many times by visiting children that they "don't eat beets." They have never eaten mine, I tell them. And sure enough, once they try just one bite of tiny, tender, freshly harvested baby beets and greens steamed lightly and served with a pat of butter, 9 out of 10 ask for more.

Given their long season of availability, culinary flexibility, and ease of cultivation, beets have a lot to offer. The season begins with the first tiny thinnings for spring salads. Next come beet greens for cooking, baby beets, mature beets for fall storage, and, finally, sprouted beet tops for tasty greens in the winter. Beets can be cooked as a vegetable, pickled as an appetizer, used as the base for marvelous soups, or served cold in salads. In the garden, they

Beets

are a dependable grower. They germinate quickly and once established are very vigorous plants.

Beets are a sensitive crop, and there is a big difference between good beets and exceptional beets. The extra care required to grow exceptional beets is repaid in the quality of roots and tops. The beet is one plant (the cabbage and onion families are others) that defines the health of garden soil. Beet leaves have a vigorous and vibrant glow when conditions in the garden approach the ideal.

Beets grow best in a nearly neutral soil. If they don't thrive it is often attributable to soil acidity. The gardener should plan to add enough lime to attain a pH of 6.5 to 6.8, a level at which most garden vegetables will do well. Beets also grow best in a soil with adequate organic matter. A generous application of compost will be well rewarded.

Beets are sensitive to deficiencies of trace elements. When beets are not sweet and tender, a lack of boron or other trace element may be the cause. Boron can be supplied by sprinkling borax *very lightly* over the soil. Trace elements can be most easily added to the soil with greensand or a dried seaweed product. A garden with plenty of organic matter from a compost of mixed ingredients usually has an adequate supply of trace elements and should present you with no difficulties in growing tasty beets.

Professional beet growers choose separate varieties for greens, baby beets, and storage. In the home garden, one all-around variety such as *Detroit Dark Red* will serve well for the whole season. Beets may be sown from January to August. Sow the earliest seeds in your cold frames. You can grow them there or transplant them to the garden. Direct sowings in the garden can be made until early August for a late-fall harvest of tender baby beets. The beet seeds you plant are actually small pods containing 2 to 3 seeds. They grow best if thinned to avoid overcrowding. Let them grow to 1½ inches tall, then use the thinnings in salads. Thin carefully so as not to disturb the roots of the plants nearby. Thin beets for greens to 2 inches apart, for summer use to 3 inches, and for winter storage to 4 inches. Rows for regular-sized beets should be 12 inches apart. If you want larger beets, plant rows 16 inches apart.

BROCCOLI   See CABBAGE FAMILY

BRUSSELS SPROUTS See **CABBAGE FAMILY**

CABBAGE FAMILY *Brassica* spp.

Planting Distance—
Broccoli: 1 row per 30-inch-wide bed; plants 16 inches apart.
Brussels sprouts: 1 row per 30-inch-wide bed; plants 18 inches apart.
Cabbage: 1 row per 30-inch-wide bed; plants 16 inches apart.
Cauliflower: 2 rows per 30-inch-wide bed; plants 16 inches apart.
*Crop Rotation—*Related to mustard, rutabagas, kale, turnips, collards, kohlrabi, and radishes. They do well after a leguminous green manure.
*Growing Tips—*Till autumn leaves into the soil in fall.
*Storage Tips—*Cool and moist. Broccoli lasts 1 week, cauliflower 2 weeks, brussels sprouts 3 weeks, and cabbage 6 to 8 months.
*Variety Tips—*Broccoli • *Emperor*
Brussels sprouts • *Widgeon*
Earliest cabbage • *Bergkabis*
Red cabbage • *Ruby Perfection*
Savoy cabbage • *Chieftain Savoy*
Cauliflower • *Cashmere*

BROCCOLI—A healthy broccoli plant is almost a perpetual vegetable. Once you cut the main head, it is followed by an endless stream of smaller subheads. These small shoots are the perfect size for any dish. When you read seed catalogs, look specifically for varieties that have "good side-shoot production." As long as you keep harvesting them, the plant will keep producing, right up until heavy winter freezes. If you provide the protection of tall cold frames or a mobile greenhouse, they will keep producing for another 6 weeks beyond that.

BRUSSELS SPROUTS—This delicious winter vegetable has an image problem. Many centuries of being one of the last green plants in the garden have made it seem a plebeian winter survival food. Well, it certainly is designed for hardiness. The stem is a storage and feeding unit for rows of miniature cabbages. The large leaves, which droop progressively as the weather cools, provide very effective winter insulation. But it also has gourmet potential. Think of all the uses for miniature cabbages.

The onset of cold weather and freezing temperatures enhances the flavor of brussels sprouts. Once the fierce cold of December arrives here in Zone 5, however, the sprouts begin to decrease in quality. At that point, you can cut the whole stem, remove the leaves, and store the stem with sprouts attached in the root cellar for up to 3 weeks. If you have grown plants where they will be covered by your mobile greenhouse, it will provide enough protection to extend the harvest at least another month and a half.

CABBAGE—Cabbage is a year-round food. It is fresh from the garden in summer and fall and fresh from the cellar in winter and spring. Well-grown cabbages in my cellar keep so successfully that we usually eat the last root cellar cabbage just prior to maturity of the first spring planting.

I favor red and savoy cabbage so much that I often don't grow the standard, round, smooth-leaved green cabbage. Red cabbage is a vigorous plant, it stores well, and it is the basis for sensational sauerkraut and cooked dishes. Savoy cabbage, with its crinkly green leaves, is by far the most flavorful of the green cabbages either cooked or raw.

CAULIFLOWER—Cauliflower is the most troublesome and least productive of the cabbage family crops. The cauliflower has only a single head, is available for only a short period, and requires tying and blanching to keep it white. The self-blanching varieties, whose leaves fold over the head to exclude most light, don't always do the job adequately. Cauliflower needs a certain amount of cool weather to initiate head formation, but early cauliflower transplants are liable to bolt and produce only small button heads when temperatures are too cool in their youth.

These remarks are not meant to disparage cauliflower. I enjoy eating it, but the difficulties of growing it are real. Many home gardeners find this crop easy to ignore because so many other vegetables offer a lot more eating for a lot less work. If you want to grow cauliflower, it is most successful as a fall crop. The cool fall temperatures keep the heads in a harvestable condition for a much longer period. You will want to start the plants about

2½ months before the first fall frost. Choose a self-blanching variety to save yourself some work. The purple and green cauliflower varieties don't require blanching and are easier to grow, but they are so similar to broccoli that I usually grow the latter instead.

I start all the cabbage family members in potting soil in the cold frame and set them out as transplants. They get off to an excellent start in the highly fertile potting soil, and this early growth carries through to their future growth. Vigorous seedlings are the foundation of vigorous plants.

I have noticed that cabbage family plants grow exceptionally well and have fewer pest problems (especially from cabbage root maggot, *Hylemya brassicae*) when soil nitrogen supplies are optimal. There are 2 simple ways to supply extra nitrogen to the soil in a form that the cabbage family will thrive on. First, you can use autumn leaves as a soil amendment. Either till under a few inches of autumn leaves in the fall or spread decomposed leaf mold and work it in shallowly. Add lime at the rate of 1 pound for every 20 square feet. The decomposition of the leaves liberates ideal quantities of nitrogen by the following spring.

A second option to give your cabbage family transplants a nitrogen shot is to plant a leguminous green manure the summer before the bed will be used for the cabbage family. Turn that growth under 2 to 3 weeks before setting out the plants. The nitrogen stored by the legumes is available to your cabbage family transplants when this green manure is incorporated into the soil.

If you still have root maggot problems despite these soil-improvement techniques, hunt out red or purple cultivars such as red cabbage, purple cauliflower, and red brussels sprouts. There seems to be some quality in the genetics of these variants that makes them much more resistant to this pest.

The other common cabbage family pest is the imported cabbage worm, *Pieris rapae,* which is the larva of the white cabbage butterfly. Although considered a common pest, these green worms are not a problem when plants are growing well. In case of need, you can use a bacterial pathogen, *Bacillus thuringiensis,* which is specific to lepidopterous larvae. It is sold under a variety of brand names (Dipel, Thuricide, and Biotrol, among others) and offers excellent control of the worm.

*Adding autumn leaves
to the soil*

CARROT   *Daucus carota*

Planting Distance—
   Cold frame crop: Rows 6 inches apart; seeds 1 inch apart; thin
      to 2 to 3 inches apart for early spring crop.
   Main crop: 3 rows per 30-inch-wide bed; seeds ½ inch
      apart; thin to 1 inch apart.
Crop Rotation—Related to parsley, celery, celeriac, and parsnips.
Growing Tips—Carrots grow well in soil where autumn leaves
   are incorporated. Benefit from the minerals in greensand.
Storage Tips—Store in root cellar at 32°F. Can be stored in soil
   with protection such as cold frame or heavy mulch.
Variety Tips—Early • *Minicor*
   Main crop • *Scarlet Nantes, Nantes Touchon*
   Overwinter • *Napoli*

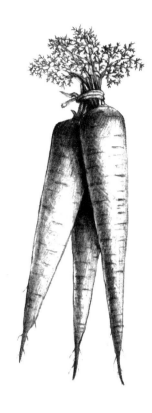

The carrot encompasses a wider range of quality and flavor characteristics than any other vegetable. Most home gardeners can grow a decent carrot, but a *decent* carrot only scratches the surface. The peaks of flavor attainable with the right variety, adequate and balanced minerals, and carefully composted soil are positively awesome.

My children come home from school with their friends and head out to the garden, the cold frame, or the tunnel, depending on the time of year, to pull and eat carrots. They weren't told to do this; they do it because the taste of the carrots is so exceptional that it has more appeal than any goodies from the cupboard or refrigerator. I have seen a similar reaction from customers, both young and old, at my market garden. Most people comment that my carrots seem to be another vegetable entirely from the pale, petroleum-tasting, bitter pseudocarrots sold in the supermarket.

And no wonder. Many studies have shown that carrots absorb and concentrate pesticide and heavy metal residues when grown in a soil containing those pollutants. Their flavor also is adversely affected by the petroleum oils used as herbicides in commercial carrot growing. Furthermore, commercial growers favor varieties with strong tops so they can withstand the tug of the harvesting machine. The juiciest and most flavorful of the marvelous French varieties can be harvested only by hand and are found only from specialist growers or in your own backyard.

Carrots respond well to the soil fertility tenets of this book: a well-decomposed, mostly vegetable compost; rock powders; and enough lime to keep the pH around 6.5. Carrots also respond well in a soil where a lot of deciduous leaves (up to 4 inches) have been incorporated with the tiller the previous fall. I have always thought that oak leaves were best in this regard, but you can use whatever is available.

Soil temperatures affect both the growth and flavor of many root crops. Carrots suffer when soil temperatures are too warm. Mulching in warm weather will improve growing conditions, but carrots are at their peak during the cooler months of the year. You can take advantage of that situation for a whole winter of delightful carrot munching by planting carrots in a cold frame on the latest date possible in your area. Here in Zone 5, that is about August 1. Put the lights on the frame in October to keep the carrots growing and protect them from hard freezes. Sometime between mid-November and mid-December, sprinkle enough compost over the bed (an inch or so) to bury them, tops and all. Then fill the frame with straw and replace the glass cover.

That frame full of small, tender carrots will be available for harvest throughout the winter in all but the coldest climates. Just lift the glass, stick your hand down through straw and compost, and pull carrots as you need them. They will be fresh, crisp, and as sweet as orange Popsicles. The cold storage in the soil changes some of the starch to sugar, and the result is carrot nirvana. These are the carrots my children love best. They call them "candy carrots."

Spreading the compost over the bed prepares the frame for planting early crops the following spring. Remove the straw as you harvest each section of carrots and replant to early hardy crops. If you will be planting small-seeded crops in the spring, I suggest one extra precaution. Cover the carrots with a sheet of plastic or fine mesh netting before you put in the straw. That way any detritus from the straw will be contained and won't require extra effort to separate from the soil before replanting.

When planting cold frame carrots or any carrots to be harvested small, you can put the rows as close as 4 inches apart. For the earliest harvest, thin the carrots to a wider spacing—2 to 3 inches apart in the row. They grow more rapidly with extra space immediately around them. I plant main crop carrots in

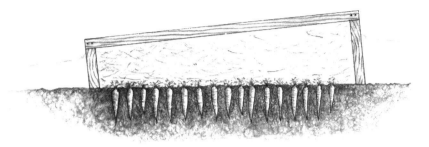

Carrots covered with a cold frame and straw mulch can be harvested all winter.

rows 10 inches apart, then I thin to 1 inch apart in the row. At harvest, I fork the soil to loosen the carrots, pull them, cut the tops to within an inch of the crown, and set them in the storage container, which goes in the root cellar. They will remain in excellent condition through May. Carrot seeds planted in an empty spot in a cold frame in December or January will usually be up by February and yield early new carrots in May to start the cycle all over again.

CAULIFLOWER   See CABBAGE FAMILY

CELERY & CELERIAC   *Apium graveolens*

Planting Distance—3 rows per 30-inch-wide bed; plants 10 inches apart.
Crop Rotation—Related to carrots, parsley, parsnips.
Growing Tips—Rich soil and plenty of water.
Storage Tips—Celery can keep for 2 months at cool temperatures. Celeriac will store all winter in the root cellar at 32°F.
Variety Tips—Celery • *Ventura*
   Celeriac • *Brilliant*

The children can learn a lot about plant breeding and selection if you show them the difference between these 2 vegetables. Whereas celery has been selected for the crispness and flavor of the stalks, the selection of celeriac (also known as knob-rooted or turnip-rooted celery) has emphasized the dense, white, rootlike matter at the base of the plant. The result of these efforts is that good celery has crisp stalks and not much base, and good celeriac has a round knob of base material and stalks that are pithy when large. Their roles are not interchangeable, but they serve admirably at what they do best.

Celery is not difficult to grow if you pay attention to 3 cultural practices. The first is soil moisture. Watering will solve more celery problems than any other practice. Celery thrives on a moist (not sodden) soil and will repay any special treatment you give it in that regard. An easy home garden practice is to mulch around the newly set out celery plants with flat rocks (flagstones or roofing tiles are excellent, as they are easy to place and remove). The stones retain both moisture and warmth.

The second key to exceptional celery is organic matter. Celery grows best in a rich soil, and that means plenty of compost or well-rotted manure. It is hard to find a soil too rich for celery. I knew an enthusiast who would collect waste eggs from a hatchery; smash them up, shells and all; dilute them with water; and pour the mixture down the rows between the celery plants. That was a rich diet, but that was also *some* celery.

Third, and in many ways the sine qua non, is seedling temperature. If you start celery indoors and transplant it to the garden when the weather is still cool, many of the plants will bolt—that is, go to seed. When 4- to 8-week-old celery plants are moved from warm indoor temperatures to spend the next 10 days or so at an average temperature below 50°F, the celery assumes it has had a summer (the warm temperatures) and winter (the cool temperatures) and is now in its second year. With globe artichokes, this same pattern, done intentionally, produces the edible part. When it happens with celery, however, the result is celery seed rather than celery stalks. You can avoid this temperature-induced bolting by waiting until average outdoor temperatures are dependably over 50°F before setting out the plants. For the earliest crop, this means transplanting them to the protection of a tunnel or cold frame.

Everything said so far about celery also applies to celeriac, only less so. Celeriac is much more forgiving. When conditions are less than perfect, celeriac will still grow admirably in the home garden. It will excel, however, and produce positively sensational roots when given the best celerylike growing conditions.

I sow both crops indoors in small flats. Celery and celeriac are slow to germinate and benefit from being kept warm and moist during the process. For lack of anything fancier, you can place the flats in a plastic bag and set them on top of the refrigerator. Check them every day and move them to a sunny spot when the seedlings emerge. I transplant the small seedlings to a wider spacing once I can distinguish enough to choose the best plants. I set them out in the bed in 3 rows 10 inches apart with the plants spaced at 10 inches in the row.

I make my earliest celery seeding around March 1, then transplant the seedlings to a cold frame or greenhouse. I start the fall crop about June 1, then transplant the seedlings to the edge bed of the mobile tunnel, where they will be protected well into the fall. I sow celeriac in April and set the plants out in June. If necessary, both celery and celeriac can remain an extra week or so in the flat as long as the potting mix is well fortified with compost, or a liquid feed such as compost tea, fish emulsion or seaweed is used.

You can harvest celery by removing the outer stalks or cutting the whole plant. If you want celery early in the season, cut some small plants. The stalks may not be large, but the flavor is just as good. Even after celery has been frosted in the fall, the inner stalks remain usable for many weeks. Protect fall celery in your mobile tunnel with a couple of layers of plastic on cold nights.

Harvest celeriac in the fall along with the other root crops. Break off the stalks, shake extra soil from the roots, and put the

Celeriac

roots in your storage container. Celeriac will keep until late the following spring. I use it to flavor soups, stews, and stir-fries. Grated raw, it complements many salads. It is especially tasty baked whole in a covered dish and served with hollandaise sauce.

CHARD   See SWISS CHARD

CHERVIL   See SALAD GREENS

CHICORY FAMILY   *Cichorium* spp.

Planting Distance—
   Endive: 3 rows per 30-inch-wide bed; plants 10 inches apart.
   Escarole: 3 rows per 30-inch-wide bed; plants 12 inches apart.
   Belgian endive: 2 rows per 30-inch-wide bed; plants 4-6 inches apart.
   Sugarloaf: Rows 10 inches apart; plants 10 inches apart.
   Italian dandelion: Rows 8 inches apart; plants 8 inches apart.
   Radicchio: 3 rows per 30-inch-wide bed; plants 10 inches apart.
   Cutting: Rows 4 inches apart; plants 1 inch apart.
*Crop Rotation—*Related to salsify, dandelion, lettuce, and globe artichokes. Generally considered a beneficial preceding crop for others.
*Growing Tips—*Vigorously growing plants that will thrive in any fertile soil.
*Storage Tips—*Store Belgian endive roots in buckets of sand as described in Chapter 8.
*Variety Tips—*Endive • *Traviata*
   Escarole • *Nuvol*
   Belgian endive • *Flash, Zoom, Robin*
   Sugarloaf • *Poncho*
   Italian dandelion • *Catalogna Special*
   Radicchio • *Giulio, Augusto, Rossa di Verona*
   Cutting • *Biondissima Trieste*

The chicory family encompasses an array of charming vegetables that are indispensable for the year-round harvest. Chicories are a shining example of the seasonal food resources this book celebrates. The Europeans have dined well from winter gardens for centuries. They had no California to ship them summer produce during the winter months, so they learned to be imaginative with what they could grow. Chicories became a staple because of their versatility. For example, endive and escarole add texture and tang to a salad; Belgian endive, or witloof as it is often called, may be served raw or cooked; the sugarloaf types of green winter chicories are used for braising and salads; Italian dandelion is planted in summer for winter and early-spring eating; the beautiful radicchio adds color and bite to cool-season salads; and the cutting varieties are a great addition to mesclun mixes.

ENDIVE & ESCAROLE—These are both slightly bitter greens and will add snap to a bland salad. Traditionally, the hearts were blanched by tying up the leaves or covering the head to make the leaves milder tasting. I find that by limiting their season to the cooler months, you can dispense with blanching, as they are not disagreeably bitter. I plant in late July to early August for a fall and winter harvest and as early in the spring as possible for a summer harvest. Escarole is the hardier of the two, but I find that the hearts of both remain edible right through most of the winter with the protection of a cold frame.

Most escarole varieties grow larger than lettuce and need to be planted at a 12-inch spacing. The *trés fine* endives have smaller heads and can be grown at lettuce spacing (10 by 10 inches) or even closer.

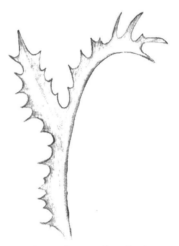

Trés fine *endive leaf*

BELGIAN ENDIVE (Witloof)—The plants you grow in the garden are the first of 2 steps in growing the edible parts of this plant. The second step is when you force the roots to get the chicons. The roots must be of good size to grow the best chicons. A diameter of 1¼ to 2 inches at the shoulder is optimal, but don't be discouraged if they are not all perfect. Even small roots will grow surprisingly vigorous chicons. Be sure to grow enough, as I have rarely met anyone who didn't find these crisp, crunchy white winter leaves to their liking. A full description of growing and storage methods can be found in Chapter 8.

SUGARLOAF—I became curious about this tall, romaine

lettuce-shaped chicory plant years ago in Europe after seeing fields of them in autumn. The cool fall weather and the natural blanching of the inner leaves by their enclosure in the outer ones removes much of the traditional chicory bitterness. Sugarloaf is a delicious green crop that survives the winter in a cold frame. Even when the outside appears frozen, brown, and mushy, there is still a tender and delicious heart inside. I stuff the outer leaves with filling, then steam or braise them. I use the inner leaves in salads by cutting the tightly wrapped hearts on an angle into thin, decorative strips.

ITALIAN DANDELION—The leaves are more tender and ready earlier in the spring than the French dandelion varieties, which are *Taraxacum* rather than *Chicorium.* Italian dandelion also grows upright, so harvesting the leaves on a cut-and-come-again basis is easier. Cut the leaves back above the crown, and they will resprout. Under the double coverage of cold frame and tunnel, the leaves are available throughout the winter. I use them in cooked dishes just like conventional dandelion or raw in a delicious Italian salad.

RADICCHIO—Radicchio is the classic Italian red chicory. The color of this vegetable is as delightful to the eye as the slightly bitter bite is to the palate. The small, round, dense heads of the *Chioggia* or *Verona* types are 2 to 5 inches in diameter. The *Treviso* types are pointed like Belgian endive. It used to be that you needed to cut back the green leaves of the summer growth in early fall to encourage the red heads to form. Those old heirloom varieties were temperamental and inconsistent headers. I still grow them for the horticultural challenge, as well as for their exceptional quality, but modern plant breeding has made radicchio easier to grow. The newer varieties, such as *Giulio, Medusa, Rossana,* and *Augusto,* do not require cutting back to initiate head formation. They are more dependable and uniform, like lettuce. That has greatly extended the season for radicchio, which can now be grown in almost any climate. Whichever type you grow, the leaves will quickly become a staple in your salad bowl.

The garden chicories are closely related to the wild chicories, which have cobalt-blue flowers and grow in fields or along the

Italian dandelion

road and bloom in midsummer. The cultivated varieties, like their vigorous weedy relatives, are no trouble to grow. They sprout quickly from seed and thrive in any fertile soil. The subtlety of their garden culture is in the timing. The gardener's main concern is timing the sowing to produce the desired result for each family member.

The first to be planted are the earliest cutting chicories for inclusion in salad mixes. They will be harvested young on a cut-and-come-again basis. Along with them, sow a spring radicchio variety and endive for early summer use. About the third week in May, I sow seeds for the roots that will be forced as Belgian endive next winter. Belgian endive is a long-season crop that won't be harvested until October. Early in June, I plant the heirloom radicchios, such as *Verona* and *Treviso,* and by early to mid-July, I start sowing Italian dandelion and the new-style radicchios that don't need to be cut back. By mid-July, I begin seeding the endive and escarole varieties for fall and winter eating.

Once the planting is done, the next subtlety is the cutting back of the heirloom radicchios so that they will have nice heads by late fall. Radicchio is very hardy, and the heads will survive for all-winter harvest in the protection of my cold frames if I can get them up to size before the weather gets too cold. I cut off the green summer leaves during the first half of September. The new growth that follows is the red radicchio. If I cut the leaves back too late, they grow very slowly in winter and are excessively bitter. This is more of an enjoyable art form than a clearly defined process, so you will have to keep experimenting with dates based on your knowledge of the variety and your assessment of the fall weather to come.

Because there is so much variety and potential with chicories, they are an adventurous crop. Over the years, I have been served chicories in Europe that went beyond what I was familiar with at the time. I know there are many more to come. As the full spectrum of this seemingly inexhaustible family is explored, new types will become available. Try them. Trying out new varieties, new techniques, and new seeds is how you learn. As a four-season gardener, you will be motivated to find additional winter crops. New chicory family seeds are an adventure waiting to happen. Start them on their way.

Radicchio

CHINESE CABBAGE   See ORIENTAL VEGETABLES

CLAYTONIA   See SALAD GREENS

CORN   *Zea mays*

Planting Distance—1 row per 30-inch-wide bed; hills of 3 plants
    1½ to 2 feet apart.
Crop Rotation—Corn grows almost anywhere with plenty of
    compost.
Growing Tips—Start a few corn seeds in pots and transplant for
    the earliest crop.
Storage Tips—Don't store. Fresh corn cannot be equaled. Sweet
    corn can, however, be blanched, cut off the ear, and dried for
    a winter treat.
Variety Tips—Early Sunglow
    Seneca Borizon
    Double Standard
    Golden Bantam
    Seneca Chief
    Sweet Sue
    Silver Queen
    Country Gentleman

As you will notice from the varieties listed, I prefer those that are either open pollinated or the original hybrids. I avoid the "sugary enhanced" or "super-sweet" types. To my taste, they were bred for the corn-selling requirements of supermarkets, not for the home garden. They may be sweet, but I think it is akin to eating sweet plastic. There is more to corn than that. The old varieties may not be as uniform or as perfect looking, but they have an honest corn flavor and are naturally sweet because I grow them in composted soil and eat them right from the garden.

Anyone who has ever found their sweet corn ravaged by hungry raccoons realizes how much these masked marauders like raw corn. You can protect your corn with a simple, lightweight electric fence (see appendix). You also may find, as I have, that the coons are on to something. Raw corn as a snack or as a meal right in the garden is my favorite way to enjoy this crop. Just pick a ripe ear, peel back the husks, and eat along the ear as you normally would. I also eat cooked corn, but I'm becoming more enamored of the raccoon style of eating the more I practice it.

I plant corn in hills down the center of a 30-inch-wide bed. I plant 4 seeds per hill and thin to 3 seedlings. I place the hills 1½ (early) to 2 (late) feet apart, which gives me an equivalent spacing of 6 to 8 inches per plant. To have corn for as long a season as possible, I purchase small packets of a half-dozen varieties with progressive maturity dates and plant a few hills of each. The extra-early varieties are often not great eating, so I get my earliest corn by starting a few hills of an early corn in 4-inch pots and transplanting them once the danger of frost has passed. Set them out shortly after they germinate (no more than 10 days old) so they don't become pot-bound. Since corn doesn't transplant easily, you need to tap the plants and root ball gently out of the pot and set them in the soil with minimal root disturbance.

I grow corn in one of the trellised beds of the garden and thus can cover the early plants with a plastic A-frame greenhouse (see Chapter 4) if I desire. I also have interplanted extra-early varieties in the spring among salad crops in a cold frame and let the corn take over once the salad crops were harvested. The lights have to be raised and eventually removed as the plants begin to push against them. To extend the season at the other end, I always plant a few hills of a very late variety. When weather conditions permit, I get a delightful late-season treat. When fall frosts come too early, I get extra material for the compost heap. Even after being frosted, however, mature corn is protected in the husks and is often edible for up to 2 weeks.

Corn is a vigorous feeder and will thrive on all the compost or manure you can provide. It can be fertilized with rougher compost than most other crops. I often put first-stage compost on the corn bed the fall before and let it finish decomposing in the soil. Like any other vigorously growing crop, corn will do best if you can provide extra moisture by irrigating in dry periods. Whatever effort you make is worth it for this crop.

CRESS　See **SALAD GREENS**

Plant corn in hills

CUCUMBER *Cucumis sativus*

Planting Distance—
   Trellis: Plants 18 inches apart.
   Ground: Plants 30 inches apart.
Crop Rotation—Related to squash and melons. Generally
   considered a good preceding crop.
Growing Tips—Add dried seaweed to the soil if you are bothered
   by cucumber beetles.
Storage Tips—Can be stored in the refrigerator for 1 week.
Variety Tips—Trellised • *Sweet Success, Lemon*
   Low-growing • *Vert de Massy*

The home garden is paradise for the cucumber lover. You can choose to grow your favorites—whether long or round, tiny or curved—and you can choose to grow them right. There seems to be a special quality to cucumbers cultivated the old-fashioned way with lots of organic matter.

In the prechemical days, professional market gardeners

Cucumber

appreciated the exceptionally fertile soil needed for superior cucumbers. I remember an afternoon spent with one of France's most experienced organic growers. When he spoke about soil preparation for cucumbers, his eyes lit up like those of a chef describing the ingredients for a classic dish. He would dig a trench in the greenhouse about 12 inches deep and the width of a straw bale. He would then lay straw bales end to end in the trench, cover them with guano and blood meal, and water the supplements in with a hose. The moisture plus the nitrogen in the guano and blood meal started the bales composting. Within a month, they were sufficiently broken down that he could cover them with soil and well-decomposed sheep manure (he specified sheep manure for cucumbers) and set out the cucumber transplants on top. The bales would continue composting slowly, thus providing a gentle bottom heat for the cucumbers, as well as plenty of organic matter. In addition to watering, he applied a compost tea once a week. The plants were trained to the roof of the greenhouse and then back down. Any cucumber lover would have genuflected.

I don't expect you to copy my French friend's system. I tell the story as a metaphor of old gardening wisdom. It celebrates the care and competence with which perceptive growers long ago learned to create biological systems. Their obvious success in optimizing the quality and flavor of their crops belies the modern myth that soil life can be replaced with lifeless chemicals.

I provide my cucumbers with all the fertility I can spare by adding extra compost and dried seaweed to the soil. The extra trace minerals enhance pest resistance. I grow cucumbers on the trellis structures described in Chapter 4 by training them up a string. I prefer a European-style trellising variety such as *Sweet Success*. I prune the plants to one stem, then remove all the shoots that form in the leaf node between the main stem and the leaf branch. After the plants are 2 feet high and well established, I allow 1 fruit to form at each node but continue to remove the other shoots. I wind the stem around the string for support as it goes up. If you don't want to prune, you can hang pea netting from the trellis and encourage all the stems and branches to weave their way upward. The netting will support the fruits. Trellised cucumbers grow long and straight, and they are easy to see and pick.

I start the cucumbers 2 weeks ahead of the safe outdoor planting date in 4-inch pots in a sunny window and transplant them down the center of the bed at an 18-inch spacing. If the early-summer weather is at all unfavorable, I turn the trellis into a temporary A-frame greenhouse as described in Chapter 4.

I extend the season both early and late by growing cucumbers under the mobile tunnel in its summer location. The late crop shares space with tomatoes, melons, beans, and New Zealand spinach. The earliest crop is a nontrellising variety that I start indoors and transplant as early as I dare. With a tender crop like cucumbers, it's wise to start a second planting a week after the first in case unseasonably cold weather sets back your first try. Pick them daily for best quality.

DANDELION *Taraxacum officinale*

Dandelion

Planting Distance—3 rows per 30-inch-wide bed; seeds 1 inch apart; thin to 6 inches apart.
Crop Rotation—Related to chicories, salsify, lettuce, and globe artichokes. Generally considered a beneficial preceding crop.
Growing Tips—Provide moist, rich soil.
Storage Tips—Will store in the refrigerator for 1 week.
Variety Tips—*Fullheart Improved*

The dandelion is a cool-weather crop and at its best in the spring. Legions of dandelion lovers go out every April to collect wild dandelion greens. For my part, I prefer to grow a cultivated variety in the garden. Cultivated varieties have large, vigorous leaves and hearts that are easy to clean. With a little protection, they can be harvested over a very long season. I sow small plantings in protected cold frames, outdoor cold frames, and the open garden so I can harvest progressively from each area in turn.

I have always enjoyed the flavor of this plant, but I would not be amiss to grow it just because it is good for me. The botanical name *Taraxacum* means "remedy for disorders" in the original Greek. The dandelion has high levels of all sorts of desirable nutrients. Herbalists can write tomes on its virtues. The French, who seem to appreciate the edible qualities of weeds, have developed larger and more delicious strains so the gardener can have all the virtues of this plant without any culinary sacrifice.

ENDIVE   **See CHICORY FAMILY**

ESCAROLE   **See CHICORY FAMILY**

GARLIC   *Allium sativum*

Planting Distance—5 rows per 30-inch-wide bed; plants 6
   inches apart.
Crop Rotation—Related to leeks, onions, shallots, and chives.
   Don't plant where cabbage family grew the year before.
   Generally considered a beneficial preceding crop.
Growing Tips—Plant in mid-October for next year's harvest.
Storage Tips—Store well-cured bulbs in cold (30s), dry place.
Variety Tips—Try a number of varieties until you find the one
   that grows best in your garden. Different garlic strains have
   specific soil and climate preferences.

Garlic

Fortunately, garlic is as easy to grow as it is indispensable in
the kitchen. The most important cultural advice is to find a
variety adapted to your conditions. Test-plant as many garlic
strains as you can and choose the one that thrives in your soil. All
that remains is to select the largest bulbs each year to be saved for
seeds.

I plant only fall garlic. I wait until mid-October, then break
the selected bulbs into cloves and plant them at 6-inch spacings.
Poke the blunt end into the ground so the pointed tip is just at
soil level. The idea is for the clove to be able to establish good root
growth but no top growth in late fall. Plant garlic where no
member of the cabbage family grew the year before. Crop
rotation trials have found that the growth and yield of onion
family members can be inhibited by as much as 60 percent
following a cabbage family crop.

In late fall, cover the bed with straw to protect the soil over
the winter. Remove the straw in spring and top dress the bed with
compost. Be sure to keep the garlic plot well weeded. Garlic is
mature when the tops fall over (mid-July to early August).
Harvest by loosening the soil with a fork and pulling up the
bulbs. Garlic must be cured after harvest to prevent decay in
storage. The ideal curing conditions are a high temperature and

high humidity with good air movement. Those conditions can be achieved outdoors in summer by placing the garlic on a homemade drying rack. You can make the simplest rack by setting a window screen across 2 sawhorses. I set the rack in the sun and move it to a porch or cover it with a tarp if rain threatens. Garlic can be considered cured when the neck is tight and the outer skin dry. You can either weave the dry tops into a braid or store the heads without tops in a net bag.

If you end up with more garlic than you need, or if you have a number of small or substandard heads, you can make a meal from them next spring. Plant them out a couple of inches apart in an unused part of the fall garden and harvest them early next year as tender, green garlic (like green onions). Trim off the roots, sauté them slowly in butter, and serve them on toast with the sauce of your choice.

HERBS

Along with vegetables, you'll certainly want to grow herbs to complement them. I'm no herb specialist, but I do grow basil, dill, savory, sage, and thyme on a regular basis for fresh use and drying. I start the annuals from seeds and divide and replant the perennials as necessary. I also grow French tarragon and rosemary outdoors in summer, but in this climate, they need to spend the winter in a sunny window. I grow peppermint and German chamomile for tea and carefully tend a lemon verbena plant for my favorite vervain tea. The latter also must spend the cold months indoors.

Drying herbs

My simple technique for drying herbs is to pick them at their best and dry them out of the sun in a warm, airy place. I tie them in small bunches and hang them from the beams in the kitchen. That's not only functional, but also beautiful and aromatic. They are dry when crisp and easily crumbled.

Perennial herbs can be transplanted into the cold frame for fresh production beyond the outdoor season. Some good bets are sage, oregano, thyme, and chives. For the coldest weather pot up a few plants and winter them inside in a sunny window.

KALE   *Brassica oleracea*

Planting Distance—2 rows per 30-inch-wide bed; plants 16 inches apart.

Crop Rotation—Related to mustard, rutabagas, collards, broccoli, cauliflower, cabbage, brussels sprouts, kohlrabi, and radishes.

Growing Tips—Leaf mold is a wonderful soil amendment for kale.

Storage Tips—Can be harvested fresh all winter in most climates even without protection.

Variety Tips—Hardiest • *Vates, Winterbor*
  Tastiest • *Red Russian*

Kale under snow cover

Since I love the winter season, I have always been fond of this cold-weather vegetable. Not only does it taste good on its own, in a casserole, or chopped into mashed potatoes with a couple of fried eggs on top, but it is also loaded with vitamins and minerals. Even if you don't use cold frames and greenhouses, you can harvest kale well beyond the growing season. If you pick it from under a snow cover in December, it will still be at its best. Many years ago, I took fresh kale along for supper on a November camping trip in the White Mountains of New Hampshire. I had more than I needed, so I tucked it in the rafters of the shelter the next morning. Two months later when I returned to the same shelter on a winter trip, the kale was still there and still edible. We threw it in the pot that night.

The hardiness of kale varieties depends to some degree on their style of growth. The taller types are not as hardy as those with the growing heart closer to the ground. *Winterbor* is the hardiest of the tall varieties. *Vates* is a very hardy lower-growing variety. The lower-growing varieties are ideal for overwintering in a cold frame, since the new leaf growth starts close to the ground and can be picked before it touches the glass.

Kale responds to the same soil conditions as the other members of the cabbage family. Either autumn leaves, leaf mold, or a preceding leguminous green manure will result in excellent growth. I start kale in early July so as to have vigorous plants for cool-season eating.

KOHLRABI   *Brassica caulorapa*

Planting Distance—Rows 8 inches apart across bed; plants 8 inches apart.
Crop Rotation—Related to mustard, rutabagas, kale, and the rest of the cabbage family.
Growing Tips—Plant only as a fall crop for best quality.
Storage Tips—Winter-storage varieties will keep for months in the cellar.
Variety Tips—White • *Kolpak*
   Purple • *Blaro*
   Storage • *Gigante*

This is a shining example of the distant relative we have never gotten to know. It is surely our loss. Kohlrabi is one of the numerous vegetable members of the cabbage family. Its Latin variant name, *caulorapa,* translates as "stem turnip," an accurate but unflattering description. Don't be put off by name or unfamiliarity. This is a wonderful winter vegetable.

There are both purple and green varieties of kohlrabi. The purple certainly looks snazzier in the fall garden and is slightly hardier, but under good growing conditions, they both taste about the same. Kohlrabi starts out like any other cabbage family seedling, but instead of growing buds, flowers, or heads, it begins to look pregnant. The swollen stem is the food-storage organ for kohlrabi. Kohlrabi can be pickled, grated raw in salads or coleslaw, cut in sticks or thin slices as a base for hors d'oeuvres, added to soups and stews, or baked whole. The standard purple and green varieties are at their best when the bulb is the size of a

Kohlrabi

tennis ball or smaller. Giant winter varieties produce tender storage kohlrabi in the grapefruit to volleyball range.

I limit my production of kohlrabi to fall and winter because it tastes better and grows to a dependable harvest size at that time of year. In the cool temperatures and shortening fall days, kohlrabi slows its growth naturally and remains crisp and tender for a long time. I grow kohlrabi outdoors in the garden until hard freezes begin. Then I harvest the remaining bulbs, trim off the leaves and stem, and store them in the cellar. Well-grown plants will store for the whole winter. I also grow this crop in cold frames under the plastic tunnel for a winter-long harvest. Kohlrabi is hardy enough to be left in the garden in Zone 6 and south. Even in those climates, the slight protection of a cold frame or plastic tunnel will keep the plants in better condition.

Kohlrabi can be sown directly or planted in a seedbed for transplanting. Sow from late July through mid-September depending on your climate. The advantage of transplants is that the preceding crop can remain in the garden for a few weeks longer. Leaf mold mixed into the top few inches of soil is the best possible preparation for kohlrabi, especially if you have had difficulty with fall crops of other cabbage family members. Otherwise, a light top dressing of compost before transplanting or after the seedlings are established will do just fine. I space kohlrabi about 8 inches apart in 8-inch rows.

LEEK *Allium porrum*

Planting Distance—3 rows per 30-inch-wide bed; plants 6 inches apart.

Crop rotation—Related to onions, shallots, garlic, and chives.

Growing Tips—Extra compost and adequate water will result in the finest leeks.

Storage Tips—Leave in the soil over the winter with protection; dig as needed.

Variety Tips—Winter • *Carina*
Bunching • *Varna*

Leeks

Leeks are a foundation crop of the winter garden because they are so hardy. They also are a classic ingredient for a good

157

meal. I feel like a participant in a culinary ceremony when I parade into the kitchen with freshly dug leeks snuggled in my basket. Leeks braised in butter often become a dinner dish all their own. They also form the basis for many of my favorite hearty winter soups. The word *porridge,* which initially meant a thick vegetable soup, is derived from *porrum,* the Latin word for leek.

This is a long-season crop. Start winter leeks in early spring in a cold frame seedbed. Transplant pencil-sized seedlings to their permanent home. Use a sharpened dowel to make holes about 6 inches deep in the soil. Drop in the young leeks and water the area. Let the holes fill naturally over time from rain or watering. Planting in holes in this fashion will guarantee you at least 6 inches of blanched white stem. That white portion is the most tender. I make the holes 6 inches apart in rows 10 inches apart. At that close spacing you can't hill up soil to blanch the stems further, so you must fill in between them with leaves or leaf mold if you want a longer blanched portion. I don't usually bother. I consider the 6 inches of underground stem to be sufficient.

For winter harvest, sow a hardy winter variety and transplant the seedlings to the edge beds of a tunnel or to a cold frame. With the tunnel in place or the lights on the frame, the leek harvest can be extended right through winter. In the coldest climates, the double coverage of tunnel and cold frame keeps the soil from freezing and makes for much easier leek harvest.

If you want to enjoy leeks all year-round, direct-sow a bunching leek variety early in the spring. These varieties are grown and harvested as if they were bunching onions. They grow to fountain pen size in 8 weeks or so. A few succession plantings will supply you with baby leeks right up to the time you start harvesting the winter crop.

LETTUCE *Lactuca sativa*

Planting Distance—
  Head: 3 rows per 30-inch-wide bed; plants 10 inches apart.
  Leaf: Rows 6 inches apart across bed; plants 1 inch apart.
Crop Rotation—Related to endive, escarole, chicory, and
  dandelion.
Growing Tips—Always use your best compost for growing

tender leafy crops such as lettuce.

Storage Tips—Harvest fresh from garden or cold frame.

Variety Tips—Early • *Black Seeded Simpson, Akcel*

Bibb • *Buttercrunch*

Butterhead • *Nancy, Sangria*

Leaf • *Waldmann's, Red Sails*

Cutting • *Lollo Rossa, Matchless*

Head • *Crispino, Calmar*

Cos • *Winter Density, Romulus, Little Gem*

Winter • *Brune d'Hiver, Blonde d'Hiver, D'Hiver de Verrières*

Lettuce

Red or green, frilly or smooth, leaf or head—the lettuce family embraces enough colors and textures to decorate anyone's salad bowl. Boston, bibb, butterhead, iceberg, Cos—the names evoke the annual lettuce parade from spring to fall. The specifics of *Simpson, Ruby, Buttercrunch, Rouge d'Hiver, Crispino, Lollo Rossa,* and *Little Gem* ring like exotic place names along the route. In my backyard trials over the years, I have grown at least 100 varieties of lettuce. Whenever I travel or visit gardeners, I buy or borrow seeds of new varieties. They are fun to test, taste, and compare.

Lettuce in the garden or on the table is like a large rose, beautiful and decorative. The fact that a plant this lovely is also the foundation for 3 seasons of salads is proof that nature is benign and generous. Those 3 seasons are spring, summer, and fall in Zone 5. In more southern areas the seasons are reversed— fall, winter, and spring. Heat-tolerant lettuce varieties may extend that period in some southern climates. I search for more cold-tolerant varieties to extend the winter season here.

The nonlettuce period in Zone 5 coincides almost exactly with official winter—December 21 to March 21. Young lettuce plants of the winter varieties will survive nicely in cold frames and grow to a harvestable size by around the third week in March. But the plants that have reached harvestable size in December can take the freezing and thawing only so long before they succumb, even in the protection of a cold frame and tunnel. Mâche, the cold-weather wonder, is my salad staple for the winter months and a delightful complement to lettuce in late fall and early spring. When the mâche season ends in April, the lettuce season is on its way again.

The easiest way to grow lettuce is to harvest young leaves. Plant leaf lettuce in short rows across the bed starting as early in the spring as you can. Make the rows 6 inches apart and sow 1 seed per inch in each row. Cut the leaves with a knife or scissors an inch above the soil starting when they are 4 inches high. Dress the soil with fine compost and water well, and the leaves will continue to grow for a second and third harvest. Alternatively, you can sow in succession every week or 10 days and replace the lettuce with some other crop after a once-over harvest.

It is not much more difficult to grow full-size lettuce if your soil is fertile. I always save my best compost for this crop. I prefer to transplant lettuce for full-sized heads, but you can direct-seed. I sow every week in potting soil in the corner of a cold frame and transplant the seedlings to the garden 10 inches apart in rows 10 inches apart. I love the look of tidy lettuce beds of different ages and varieties.

The planting period between early August and late September is crucial for extending the lettuce harvest into the fall. The weekly succession plantings no longer apply because lettuce growth slows down in the fall as the days shorten. I sow my fall cold frame lettuce from early August through early September. Those seedlings are transplanted to outdoor cold frames and to tunnel-covered frames for maturity during October through December. I eat my last lettuce from the tunnel-covered frames around the first day of winter.

For the earliest spring harvest, I start lettuce the last 2 weeks of September. I use hardy varieties that will winter over as small plants. I sow seeds around September 21 and again 5 to 7 days later in case the fall is especially warm and the first planting grows too large. During the shortening fall days, that brief delay between plantings has a major effect on the eventual growth before winter. I transplant the young lettuce plants (ideally no more than 3 inches in diameter) to cold frames in late October at a 6-by-6-inch spacing to allow for losses. I put them in both the tunnel-covered frames and the outdoor frames to extend the harvest season in spring. (The tunnel-covered frames mature first.) I also plant lettuce seeds in the tunnel frames in January and February, and by early May, when the overwintered crop is finished, I'm eating the first of the new spring crop.

MÂCHE or CORN SALAD   *Valerianella locusta*

Planting Distance—Rows 4 inches apart across bed; seeds 1 inch apart.

Crop Rotation—Not related to any other crop.

Growing Tips—Prepare a flat seedbed by tamping lightly with the back of a rake.

Storage Tips—Harvest mâche fresh as you need it.

Variety Tips—Vit, D'Etampes

Mâche is to winter what sweet corn is to summer—a plant adapted to its season. The mâche plant is not imposing like corn; it's just a small rosette of tender leaves each about the size of your thumb. But it is so cold resistant that it deserves coronation as the definition of vigor and robustness. Mâche is truly the winter wonder green.

Many years ago, after I first became acquainted with the cold-weather salad potential of this crop, I felt like Johnny Mâche Seed. I told friends about it and served it to guests. I planted it everywhere. It exceeded my expectations. It is not only delicious to eat but will survive and continue to grow in colder weather than any other vegetable. Like lettuce, it is a green around which the rest of a salad can be created. I was first introduced to mâche in France, and I have always called it by its French name. In English, it's known as corn salad or lamb's lettuce, and in German it's *Feldsalat*. Originally, it was a winter weed in grain fields and was harvested wild for salads long before it was domesticated.

Mâche can be grown in spring and summer, but I prefer it as a winter crop. I plant mâche in cold frames from early September through early November. It germinates best in cool soil. Mâche seeds can be sown in rows or broadcast lightly wherever there is an open space. Mâche grows an extensive network of very fine sodlike roots that stabilize the soil and make mâche almost impervious to frost heaving. Mâche also is perfect as a companion crop. For example, in the fall cold frames where lettuce, endive, or radishes are growing, I sprinkle mâche seed next to, between, and underneath those crops. It germinates in their shade, and once they are harvested, I have a lush bed of mâche to eat through the winter. I do the same under frame crops that die back during the coldest months, such as Swiss chard, sorrel, parsley, and dandelion. By the time they start growing again in spring, I have harvested the mâche.

Although it can survive outdoors, mâche is best for winter eating when protected by a cold frame or other cover. This is also true in milder climates, if only to keep winter rains from splattering soil on the small plants. Outdoor plantings of mâche will extend the harvest into April after the mâche in the frame is harvested or has begun to go to seed.

The mâche growing in the cold frames provides salads throughout the winter. No matter how cold the climate, any day that the temperature in the frame goes above freezing, mâche is ready to harvest—even if it was -20°F the night before. You can harvest mâche when the leaves are frozen if you don't mind them wilting a little in the salad bowl.

The preferred harvesting technique is to cut the whole plant at soil level. It is important to smooth and flatten the seedbed before planting mâche so that when you run your knife on top of the soil and under the leaves, you won't be piling lumps of soil onto the newly harvested plants. If you harvest progressively along each row, you will open up space for the earliest plantings of next spring's frame crops. Before planting a succession crop after mâche, it helps to add some extra nitrogen to the soil. Spread some dried blood or fish emulsion at the rate recommended on the container and mix it in. The extensive root system of mâche leaves a lot of fiber in the soil. Some extra nitrogen will allow the new crop to grow while the soil is simultaneously breaking down the mâche roots.

After harvesting, wash the mâche lightly and remove any remaining roots. (There shouldn't be any roots if you harvested right at soil level.) Mâche plants are usually served intact in a salad without being cut up. You can harvest them at any size. Smaller plants are usually more tender but not enough so to make a major difference. A mâche plant generally won't get any bigger than 4 inches in diameter, so don't postpone harvesting in anticipation of something the size of a head of lettuce. Since mâche is small, you can plant it in close rows (4 inches apart) or even broadcast the seeds. I cover the seeds lightly, with about ¼ inch of soil. Ideally, you want 1 seed per inch in the row. Mâche is so vigorous that it will produce well even if you plant closer, but

Harvesting mâche

overcrowding will cause the lower leaves to yellow due to lack of light.

Mâche is my principal salad ingredient during the winter. You can mix mâche with any of the additions usually incorporated in your lettuce salads, or you can explore the unique culinary possibilities of mâche itself. My favorite is the way I first enjoyed it in France years ago—small, whole mâche plants mixed with slices of cold cooked beets, whole leaves of Belgian endive, and a light vinaigrette. Accompany that salad with an omelet of fresh duck eggs and a homemade cider from the apple orchard behind the garden, and you have the makings of a memorable meal.

MELON   *Cucumis melo*

Planting Distance—1 row per 30-inch-wide bed; plants 16 inches apart.
Crop Rotation—Related to cucumbers, watermelon, and squash.
Growing Tips—Melons need rich soil. Use plenty of compost and some dried seaweed. Warm the soil with infrared-transmitting plastic mulch.
Storage Tips—Store ripe melons for 2 weeks in the refrigerator.
Variety Tips—Cantaloupe • *Gold Star*
Charantais • *Flyer, Savor*

I will admit to excesses in regard to melons. There are entire days in August and September when my diet consists wholly of melons. I pluck them from the vine and eat gluttonously, teeth nibbling flesh off thin slices and juice dripping down my chin. Garden-ripe melons are the quintessential nectar of the gods.

I probably appreciate melons all the more because they are not easy to grow where I live. They are heat lovers, and the New England climate can be cool even in summer. Thus, I start melons indoors about 3 weeks before the frost-free date. I prewarm the soil in the melon bed by covering it with infrared-transmitting plastic (see appendix) at this time. The plastic allows the sun to warm the soil as much as possible, but it does not permit weed growth. I cut a small hole in the plastic at each spot where the melon transplants will be set out.

Melons on plastic mulch.

After transplanting, I cover the bed with a lightweight floating cover (see appendix) to provide the warmest growing conditions. I pay close attention to plant growth in the following weeks, and when the female blossoms begin to open and need to be pollinated by bees, I remove the cover. The melons then grow uncovered for the rest of the season.

I recommend both the standard American cantaloupe and the smaller, more aromatic French Charantais melons. They grow similarly, but harvesting is different. Cantaloupes are picked at what is called *full slip*—that is, when the end of the stem slips away from the melon under slight thumb pressure. If you wait that long with the Charantais, they will be too ripe. They must be picked at *leaf turn*—when the small leaf at the end of the stem next to the melon fades from green to pale tan.

My love affair with ripe melons is a metaphor for the four-season garden. Melons are available at their vine-ripened best for only 6 weeks of the year in Zone 5, but they are the best-tasting melons anyone could imagine. I have melon memories from those 6 weeks that last until the next season comes around. Against those memories, the green-picked, hard-fleshed, out-of-season supermarket melons offer nothing but disappointment.

MIZUNA   See **SALAD GREENS**

MUSTARD   See **SALAD GREENS**

NEW ZEALAND SPINACH   See **SPINACH**

ONION *Allium cepa*

Planting Distance—3 rows per bed 10 inches apart; seeds 1 inch apart; thin to 4 inches apart. Multiplants (see p. 86) are set 3 rows per bed, plants 12 inches apart.

Crop Rotation—Related to leeks, garlic, and chives.

Growing Tips—Spread lime to counteract soil acidity. Keep well weeded when young.

Storage Tips—Harvest promptly at maturity. Cure as instructed. Store in cold (32°–35°F), dry place. Protect from freezing.

Variety Tips—Main crop • *Norstar, Copra*
  Overwinter • *Walla Walla Sweet*
  Perennial • *Egyptian* or *Top Set Onion*
  Scallion • *Evergreen Hardy White*

The gardener has 3 options for planting onions: seeds, transplants, and sets. My preference is to sow onion seeds during March in a cold frame and then transplant the seedlings to the garden. Growing from seed allows me access to the full range of varieties available—red, yellow, or white; sweet or snappy; round or long. I also think this process ensures the best harvest and storage qualities. Seeds also can be sown directly in the garden if you use one of the shorter-season varieties. Some gardeners purchase transplants from the southern plant growers who advertise in garden magazines every spring. Onions transplant well, so this option is popular. Selection, however, is limited. The third and easiest option is onion sets. These are miniature onions about the diameter of a nickel or dime that were grown the fall before under crowded conditions that temporarily stunted their growth. They are easy to plant and they start growing again quickly to produce full-sized onions. The variety selection with sets is even more limited than with transplants. Also, most set onions have a flattened globe shape. This shape, compared with round onions, results in fewer slices for the effort of peeling.

I have often heard that onions want the richest soil in the garden. I agree up to a point. Onions want a very fertile soil, but they thrive on balance rather than excessive richness. Finished compost with attention to soil minerals and pH are the keys to that balance. The onion crop is a good measure of your soil-building progress. When your soil fertility is on the right track, onion foliage has a fresh look with a blue-green bloom, and the bulbs dry consistently after harvest to a tight top and well-colored skin. It may take 3 to 5 years to achieve that balance depending on the condition of the soil when you begin. I'm sure you will agree that the effort is worthwhile once you see how well onions can grow.

I find that onions do best when planted where lettuce or squashes grew the year before. Onions are seriously disadvantaged by a preceding cabbage family crop. Both my experience and 50 years of crop rotation studies at the University of Rhode Island confirm that observation. Onions and their relatives have a beneficial effect on all crops following them in the rotation.

Onions need to be cured at harvest for successful storage. Pull the bulbs when the tops fall over and leave them to dry in the sun for a day with the roots on top. Place them on a drying rack (see garlic) until the neck is tight and the outer skin is dry and rustling. I cut the tops an inch above the bulb and place the bulbs in net bags. If you keep them in a cold, dry place where they won't freeze (such as an unheated porch or attic), they will remain in good condition right through until spring.

You can bridge the gap between the last of the stored onions and the new crop in a number of ways. First, you can eat the

Curing onions

sprouts that grow on onions toward the end of their storage period. They are just as tasty as green onions, so there is no sense discarding them. Second, you can maintain a patch of the perennial *Egyptian* or *Top Set Onion* variety (*Allium cepa proliferatum*) and in fall plant out the small onion bulbs or top sets that are found on the stalks. They are hardy and will produce green onions early the following year. Third, you can plant a hardy perennial scallion such as *Evergreen Hardy White,* which will survive the winter. Fourth, you can purchase onion sets as soon as they are available in the spring and plant them to use as green onions. Plant some in the cold frame and more in the garden for a continuous harvest. Fifth, you can sow an over-wintering onion such as *Walla Walla Sweet* in a cold frame. I sow on August 1, and they survive the winter in the protection of the frame. I thin them progressively to a 4-inch spacing in late winter for use as green onions. The remaining plants produce large bulbs in July, well ahead of normal onion harvest.

ORACH   See SALAD GREENS

ORIENTAL VEGETABLES

The early botanists who roamed the deserts and mountains looking for new plant varieties were referred to as plant explorers. You can become a plant explorer without even leaving home if you grow Oriental vegetables. I was inspired to begin learning more about these crops recently when I looked through a manual on the full range of Oriental vegetables. I was amazed by the variety of vegetables Oriental gardeners have cultivated for centuries. It was like discovering another galaxy of vegetable crops in parallel with the mostly Occidental crops with which I am familiar.

When I grow a new crop, it is mainly a trial-and-error operation. The experience of putting the crop in the ground and watching what happens is my best teacher. I begin with common sense and intuition. If the crop is related to one of the plant groups with which I am familiar, I assume it will benefit from similar conditions. If it's an herb, I obviously won't plant as much as I might for a main crop. If it's a vine, I try to find a spot

Chinese cabbage

in a trellised row. Sometimes I haven't a clue. Mainly I sow them here and there around the garden and wait to see what happens. I use compost to enrich the soil. I plant short rows. If they fail, it's no loss; I just replant to something else. Even then, if there are seeds left in the packet, I'll try the crop again next year just in case the failure was an anomaly (and also because, like most gardeners, I hate to admit that there is something I can't grow).

Many lesser-known Oriental crops may be valuable additions to the winter garden. I do not have enough experience with them at the moment to do more than encourage you to experiment. But there is one Chinese cabbage I can recommend—a hybrid Napa type called *Summertime*. It can be direct-sown, but I prefer to transplant seedlings at 2 rows per 30-inch-wide bed with 16 inches between plants. *Summertime* grows well from a mid-summer planting, so it is perfect as a succession crop after a spring crop. Best of all, it will store in the root cellar for 3 to 4 months.

PARSLEY *Petroselinum crispum*

Planting Distance—
   Cold frame crop: Rows 6 inches apart; plants 6 inches apart.
   Main crop: Rows 8 inches apart; plants 8 inches apart.
*Crop Rotation—*Related to carrots, celery, and parsnips.
*Growing Tips—*Parsley can be transplanted if started in small pots.
*Storage Tips—*Dried parsley has many uses.
Variety Tips—Darki, Krausa, Italian Dark Green

Parsley is a first-rate food and should be considered as more than a garnish. I like it so much that I graze on parsley whenever I am in the garden. Parsley is the essence of garden green: it settles the stomach, cleanses the blood, refreshes the palate, and piques the taste buds. Parsley is a chlorophyll tonic and a carotene powerhouse all rolled into one delightful nibble. When grown in a fertile, humus-rich soil and given adequate moisture, parsley will be sweet and tender, with no biting aftertaste.

I once visited an organic farm in Holland that grew 10 acres of parsley for a company producing dried seasonings. The company chose this farm because its fertile soil grew such a sweet parsley. How does one harvest 10 acres of parsley? The Dutch farmer had a special machine similar to a grain combine that cut and collected the parsley as it moved down the field. You may not need 10 acres of parsley in your home garden, but when it's well grown, you will agree that it deserves more than just an out-of-the-way spot.

Since I am such a fan of parsley, I like to have it available year-round. I plant it in both the outdoor garden and the cold frames. I also pot up some plants in the fall to grow in a sunny window. Parsley seeds are slow to germinate. I sow a few seeds every so often in cold frames or corners of the garden whenever I am sowing other crops. That way, my favorite grazing green is always nearby.

PARSLEY ROOT (HAMBURG PARSLEY)—A close relative is parsley root (or Hamburg parsley), a root crop bearing the same relation to parsley as celeriac does to celery. It responds to the same cultural conditions as parsley and is grown as easily as carrots or parsnips. Parsley root complements or substitutes for other root crops in any recipe. It can be grated raw in salads, baked whole in a covered dish (my favorite), added to a shish kebab, cooked tempura style, or, the children's favorite, sliced thinly and fried for some of the best-tasting "chips" you will ever

Parsley root

eat. In winter, if there is no other source of parsley, I bring a few parsley roots up from the basement and force them in a pot on the windowsill. They will produce a continuous harvest of flat-leaved parsley for 6 weeks or more before needing to be replaced.

I plant root parsley in rows 10 to 12 inches apart and thin the plants to 6 to 8 inches apart. I dig the root parsley in the late fall and store it in the cellar. You also can leave the plants in the ground with protection so they can be dug fresh in the spring. You can harvest leaf parsley a sprig at a time or by cutting the whole bunch. Either way, the plant will continue to grow.

PARSNIP *Pastinaca sativa*

Planting Distance—Rows 12 inches apart across beds; seeds 1 inch apart; thin plants to 4 inches apart.
Crop Rotation—Related to carrots, parsley, and celery.
Growing Tips—Be sure to plant early enough to get good-sized roots. Fertilize with leaf mold.
Storage Tips—Leave in garden over the winter. Harvest when soil thaws in the spring.
Variety Tips—*Cobham Improved Marrow*

Parsnips are the hardiest of root crops. They are traditionally planted in early June for consumption the following spring. They will winter over in the soil with no protection in even the coldest climates. You can dig them once the soil thaws sufficiently. Parsnips taste very sweet in spring because the cold winter temperatures cause the roots to change some of the starch to sugar.

Parsnips are a surprisingly versatile vegetable and far more interesting eating than their pedestrian reputation may suggest. What makes them exciting is that they are suddenly available at the lowest ebb of the vegetable year—the end of winter. My favorite recipe is an equal mix of puréed parsnips and carrots with cream and a hint of nutmeg. Everyone will come back for seconds.

One spring I was inspired to celebrate the potential of this vegetable by making an all-parsnip meal. It began with an appetizer of some thinly sliced parsnips cooked like potato chips and served with a dip. That was followed by a dish using parsnips instead of potatoes in a scalloped potato recipe. Next came a palate cleanser of very thin slices (from the top of a large parsnip) fried lightly in butter to soften them and then rolled around a layer of raspberry sorbet. The main course was a vegetarian nut cutlet with cooked parsnips as a major ingredient. The meal was topped off with a parsnip pie using mashed parsnip instead of pumpkin in a standard pumpkin pie recipe. The only thing missing was the the delicate golden parsnip wine so prized by home vintners. Everyone agreed that if my culinary skills had matched my imagination, it could have been a masterpiece.

I plant parsnips in early June in rows 12 inches apart across the bed and thin the plants to 4 inches apart. A small section at the end of a bed will yield enough for spring meals. If the rest of the bed is planted to other wintered-over crops such as dandelion, salsify, sorrel, and spinach, you could place a movable cold frame over the entire bed in early spring to advance the harvest. Parsnips grow well given the same conditions as carrots. In fall, you don't have to do anything but let the tops die back naturally as the weather gets colder.

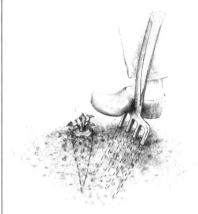

Parsnips can benefit from staying in the soil all winter.

PEAS *Pisum sativum*

Planting Distance—2 rows, 4 to 6 inches apart, down the center of a 30-inch-wide trellised bed.

Crop Rotation—Related to other legumes of the pea and bean family.

Growing Tips—Spread compost the fall before. Sow early and mulch before the weather gets hot.

Storage Tips—Don't store. This is a classic fresh vegetable.

Variety Tips—Early • *Daybreak*
Maincrop • *Lincoln*
Fall • *Maestro*
Sugar snap • *Sugar Ann, Sugar Snap*

If you have never picked a plump, green pea pod, zipped it down the seam, and popped the sweet peas into your mouth, that is reason enough to start a garden. Fresh peas are truly the king of vegetables. Even if you limit yourself to the standard round green peas (English peas to a southerner), they are regal. If you branch out into sugar snaps and snow peas, you have a whole royal family. No other crop, not even sweet corn, so perfectly defines the advantages of the home garden: food at its best when picked immediately before eating and available to snack on whenever you walk by.

I start the earliest peas in a cold frame, where I have harvested the previous crops selectively so as to open up a 10-inch-wide strip along the inside back wall. I plant the peas in that strip in two parallel rows about 4 to 6 inches apart. They eventually grow up either side of a short trellis that I erect later. In frames, I plant the variety *Daybreak* because it is very early. Since I'm using the cold frame, I can plant a month or two earlier than I could outdoors. By the time the peas grow tall enough to reach the glass, the weather is usually safe to slide the frames back and let the peas grow through. I then build a 3-foot-tall version of the trellis described in Chapter 4 with an upright at either end and a crossbar holding the netting. If for some reason I need to close the frame after this point, I raise the lights and lean them against the crossbar, then cover the back side with plastic or any other temporary protection.

It is possible to get a harvest even sooner with one of the extra-early sugar snap varieties such as *Sugar Ann.* Since sugar snaps are usable at all stages, you can eat the pods like snow peas almost as soon as they form.

Peas

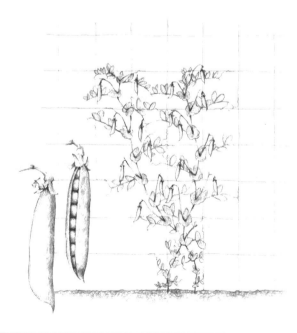

The main crop of peas in the outdoor garden is planted in two parallel rows 4 to 6 inches apart down the center of one of the trellised beds. "As early as the ground can be worked" is an old refrain in garden jargon, but it's good advice. Peas are a cool-weather crop, and the yield and quality are best from an early-spring planting. If you have mixed some compost into the soil the fall before, all that remains in early spring is to drop in the seeds. When the peas are up and growing well, I mulch the bed 4 inches deep with hay or straw. That keeps the soil cooler and moister, lengthening the pea harvest.

The traditional advice for spacing rows of trellised peas is to put them as far apart as the peas are tall. For peas with 6-foot-tall vines, that means a 6-foot row spacing. Those spacings are sound advice on a commercial basis, but the home gardener can close things up somewhat. In my garden, the 30-inch-wide bed is perfectly fine for even the tallest peas if I keep the vines from billowing out too far. I control billowing by running garden twine horizontally outside the vines to hold them against the trellis netting. I put up a new strand every foot or so as the peas grow. You also can reduce billowing by planting the seeds farther apart in the parallel rows so there is less plant mass looking for growing space. English gardeners have traditionally planted pea seeds farther apart than Americans. You will determine the best seed spacing for specific varieties by experience, but most peas (especially *Lincoln,* my favorite) grow very well at 2 inches apart in the row, and some of the taller ones grow well at up to 4 inches apart.

In addition to green shell peas, I also grow sugar snaps. If you pick the sugar snap pods when young and flat, they make very acceptable snow peas. For the sweetest sugar snaps, let them grow until the pods are filled out. I grow the original tall *Sugar Snap* variety because I like its quality. Some of the new lower-growing varieties also are acceptable.

The most impressive peas I ever grew were the result of too much of a good thing: horse manure. The pea field had been manured twice by mistake. The peas were awesome. The result surprised me because I had always considered peas to be self-feeders for nitrogen, since they are legumes. I have noticed many times, however, that peas appreciate generous manuring. The same goes for dry beans. Extra organic matter results in absolutely impeccable quality. In the garden, I apply a healthy dose of rough compost to the pea beds the fall before and let it finish its decomposition in the soil. I also inoculate the peas with the proper legume bacteria.

Whereas sugar snaps are sweetest when the pods are completely filled, I pick regular peas at 75 to 90 percent full. If you let them fill completely, they taste starchy and are harder than young peas. When peas are at their prime, they are the most irresistible vegetable in the garden. I find it difficult to get them to the kitchen because I eat so many as I pick. Usually I just give up all pretense and hunker down in the pea patch to do some serious munching. In fact, until the raw sweet corn is available, raw peas are my favorite summer meal.

You can extend the season into the fall by making a midsummer planting of peas. My traditional date for fall pea planting has been July 12 to 15. That's about 60 days before the average first light frost. Although peas are known as a hardy spring crop, only the leaves and vines are really hardy, not the pods. The first light fall frosts are no problem, but a few degrees of freezing will damage the pods. I grow my fall peas on a trellis, where I can cover them with a plastic sheet to make a temporary A-frame greenhouse as necessary (see page 57). That way, I can extend the harvest by 3 weeks or a month. *Maestro* is an excellent fall variety. One of the lower-growing sugar snap types also will fit in well here. Either way, be sure to choose a variety with resistance to pea diseases. The stress of the weather makes peas more disease prone in fall than in spring.

PEPPER *Capsicum annum*

Planting Distance—2 rows per 30-inch-wide bed; plants 18 inches apart.

Crop Rotation—Related to eggplant, potatoes, and tomatoes.

Growing Tips—Mulch with stones or infrared-transmitting plastic (see appendix) in cool climates.

Storage Tips—Sweet peppers will keep for 2 to 3 weeks in the refrigerator. Hot peppers are easily dried.

Variety Tips—Earliest • *Ace*
   Tastiest • *Lipstick*
   Hot • *Caliente*

Peppers

Recently, plant breeders have lent their talents to liberating the range of colors that exist in pepper genes. Whereas most peppers are green when immature, the rainbow of colors starts as they ripen. Catalogs now offer brown, yellow, purple, orange, white, and tan, as well as the traditional red. Hot pepper lovers have always sought to liberate the wide range of hot, hotter, and hottest that peppers can attain. All those options are available in the specialty seed catalogs. Most sweet and hot peppers can be grown with success even in the upper latitudes.

If you live in a cool coastal or northern climate, you can grow sweet and hot peppers under the mobile tunnel. Greenhouse peppers are common in Europe and are pruned like tomato plants, with the stems tied to overhead supports for vertical growth. The eventual production is enormous. In the outdoor garden, growth can be enhanced by using the same flat stone mulching technique that conserves soil moisture around celery. The stone mulch absorbs heat to warm the soil and air around the peppers. Once the plants are large enough to shade the stones, the extra heat is no longer needed. The moisture-conserving properties continue to operate for the entire season.

If you start your own pepper plants, prune off any blossoms that form while they are still in pots. You will lose a little early production, but the plants will be much more vigorous. You can increase total yield by continuing that pruning technique after the peppers are in the garden. If you continue to snip off the earliest blossoms before the fruits form, thus allowing the plant to become established before it has to support fruits, the eventual yield will be higher because later production will increase. In a New England trial, the highest total pepper yield came from plants whose blossoms were removed until July 1. Those plants were able to put all their early energy into growing a vigorous root system, which then supported greatly increased pepper production for the rest of the summer.

Set out pepper plants 18 inches apart in 2 rows 18 inches apart. Fertilize the bed with well-decomposed compost. Don't use leaves or leaf mold. The extra nitrogen they supply encourages the plants to go more to leaf than to fruit, and the yield will be greatly reduced even though the plants may look spectacularly large.

Sweet peppers are eaten fresh while the season lasts. Late fruits picked before the first frost will remain in edible condition for 2 weeks or more if kept cool (50°F) and moist. The small hot peppers are a natural crop for drying. I pull the whole plant and hang it by the stem in a sunny shed. If the weather is too moist, I hang them from the beams in the kitchen along with the herbs.

PLANTAIN   See SALAD GREENS

POTATO *Solanum tuberosum*

Planting Distance—1 row per 30-inch-wide bed; plants 12 inches apart.
Crop Rotation—Related to tomatoes, peppers, and eggplant.
Growing Tips—Plant 3 inches deep. As soon as shoots emerge, spread 1 inch of rough compost and mulch 6 to 8 inches deep with straw.
Storage Tips—Always store in darkness. Potatoes keep best at 40°F. Below 38°F, they tend to become undesirably sweet.
Variety Tips—White • *Charlotte, Kennebec*
Red • *Rideau*

Potatoes have not been as common a home garden crop as one would expect. There seems to be an assumption that they belong on a farm. Fortunately, that misconception is changing. Home gardeners have learned that potatoes are easy to grow and very productive. But there is one serious problem with growing your own. Potatoes grown in a fertile, well-com-posted soil will taste so good that you will never again be satisfied with store-bought potatoes. It is similar to what I mentioned earlier with carrots. Homegrown potatoes seem like a whole new vegetable.

A lot of potatoes can be grown in a very small space. The home garden yield from a 30-foot row should be about 60 pounds (1 bushel). That's pretty good, since the average per capita per year consumption in the United States is 2 bushels. Even if you can't find the space to grow all your potatoes, at least grow some for the joy of tasting a real potato. You may then be inspired to search out a local organic farmer from whom you can buy extra potatoes every fall.

Another delight of growing your own is the wide variety available. One outgrowth of the present interest in preserving old vegetable seeds has been an increased availability of old-time potatoes. Catalogs now list more than 100 cultivars, covering every conceivable skin color, flesh color, texture, flavor, and use (see appendix). It is definitely worth trying a number of potatoes to find the ideal variety for your soil and taste preference.

Growing potatoes couldn't be easier. What you eat is what you plant. You can purchase seed potatoes to plant, or if you have healthy crops, you can plant your own. If after a year or two yields decline or the foliage looks odd, you may again wish to buy new certified seed potatoes from the specialty growers in northern areas.

There are many systems for growing potatoes. I use a combination of practices for the best results. I plant small, whole seed potatoes 3 inches deep and 12 inches apart in a single row down the center of a 30-inch-wide bed. When the first sprouts poke through the soil, I spread an inch of rough compost and mulch the entire bed 6 to 8 inches deep with straw. I renew the mulch as needed during the summer if it looks thin.

straw over the bed

Mulching benefits potatoes by keeping the soil cooler and moister. I have found that the major potato pest, the Colorado potato beetle *(Leptinotarsa decemlineata)* can be controlled more simply and successfully by mulching than by any other single practice. The major stresses on potatoes during growth seem to arise from inadequate moisture and excessive soil temperature. A thick mulch is the most effective way of lessening temperature and moisture stress, thus enhancing the plant's resistance.

I often plant a few potatoes for extra-early harvest in one of the cold frames. I put the seed potatoes in a warm room for a month before my planting date to encourage them to begin sprouting. The early sprouting results in faster growth after planting and earlier harvest. If you are hungry for early potatoes and don't wish to dig the whole plant, you can sneak your hand into the soil around the roots and steal a potato or two. This practice is traditionally called grabbling.

I grow potatoes in the same garden where I grow the rest of my vegetables. I do not segregate them to an acidic soil to minimize the potato scab problem, as so many gardening books recommend. A potato adapted to my soil and carefully tended will grow exceptional crops with little or no scab at a pH of 6.5 to 6.8. With potatoes, as with other crops, the optimal soil levels of organic matter, minerals, moisture, and aeration are the keys to successful culture.

PUMPKIN   See SQUASH FAMILY

PURSLANE   See SALAD GREENS

RADICCHIO   See CHICORY FAMILY

RADISH   *Raphanus sativus*

Planting Distance—
  Small: Rows 4 inches apart across bed; seeds 1 inch apart.
  Large storage-type: Rows 10 inches apart; seeds 1 inch apart; thin to 6 inches apart.
Crop Rotation—Related closely enough to the cabbage family that it is best not to precede or follow those crops with radishes.
Growing Tips—Best if grown quickly. Amend soil with compost and leaf mold. Keep well watered.
Storage Tips—Winter types store until spring at 32°F. Small radishes will keep for a few weeks in the refrigerator, but they are best fresh.
Variety Tips—Small • *Sora, D'Avignon*
  Daikon • *Miyashige*
  Winter • *Round Black Spanish*

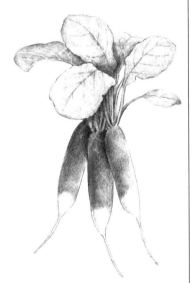

French Breakfast *radishes*

I remember the snack I was served on a recent visit to Europe. I was talking with one of Germany's best organic growers. On the table were platters of red and white radishes in different shapes and sizes interspersed with curly green parsley, thick slices of yellow cheese, and brown bread. The platters were surrounded by steins of a local organic dark beer. The warm browns, yellows, and reds not only set a beautiful table but also enhanced the warmth and camaraderie of the discussion that followed.

I remember another radish scene, this time at a small

intensive market garden south of Paris. It was a misty day, and 2 workers were harvesting and bunching *French Breakfast* radishes (lovely, oval-shaped bright red radishes with a white tip). They laid each bunch on the soil behind them as they proceeded. The artistic trail of radish bunches with bright green tops and red and white roots looked like a French Impressionist painting. And well it should have. Radishes provide not only good eating but also culinary art. They decorate the table with a beauty that aids digestion.

The radish is a far more versatile vegetable than many people imagine. It is traditionally the first crop harvested from the earliest spring planting and the last that can be sown for a late-fall harvest. Radishes vary in size from the small red radishes common in stores to the massive round or tubular Oriental types. They span every color in the chromatic range, including white and black. They can be eaten raw, cooked, or pickled. When they go to seed, the seedpods are delicious, and the seeds can be sprouted for a snappy addition to midwinter salads.

Radishes grow best in cool, moist conditions. This makes them a fall, winter, and spring vegetable in most of the country. For crisp, sweet roots, they must be grown quickly so as to prevent any check to their growth. First, make sure the soil has plenty of organic matter. Second, water them if the soil gets dry. Radishes like full sun, but they will grow well as an interplanted crop.

If your soil is not yet fertile enough to liberate nutrients at the rate radishes need them, you may find radishes difficult to grow well. There are two simple solutions. First, you can plant radishes following a leguminous cover crop such as clover. This gives them extra nitrogen from the nodules and decomposing foliage of the clover. Second, you can spread autumn leaves up to 4 inches deep where you want to grow radishes the next spring. (If your soil pH is below 6, add lime.) Till the leaves into the soil or chop them in with a hoe. In the spring, till or chop again before planting. They should look fairly well decomposed. The leaves begin to break down in the soil over the winter, and by spring their nutrient release is perfect for radishes. The late-summer plantings of radishes will benefit from an inch or two of leaf mold worked into the top few inches of the soil. When soil nutrient release is ideal for radishes, you should have no problem with root maggot. If this still doesn't work for you, grow your spring and fall radishes under the protection of one of the floating fabric covers (see appendix) that has holes small enough to prevent the entry of the fly that lays the maggot eggs.

I plant small radishes in odd spots around the garden. Any open area or gap in a row is waiting for radish seeds. The rows can be as close as 4 inches apart with the plants 1 inch apart. For best quality, harvest as soon as they are ready. I plant the larger radishes in 10-inch rows at whatever spacing is appropriate for their eventual size (about 6 to 8 inches for the daikon and winter types). At harvest, I treat them like any other root crop: I pull them, top them, and store them. They keep well until May.

RUTABAGA *Brassica napus*

Planting Distance—2 rows per 30-inch-wide bed; seeds 1 inch apart; thin to 4 to 6 inches apart.
Crop Rotation—Related to the other cabbage family members.
Growing Tips—Sow after June 21. Leaf mold is the ideal fertilizer.
Storage Tips—Leave in the ground until hard frosts threaten. Store in root cellar.
Variety Tips—Pike, Gilfeather

Rutabaga

This is a sturdy vegetable. It is not fancy, and I have never tried to pretend that it is. I use it as a dependable winter staple. In addition to being an ingredient in soups, stews, and boiled dinners, I favor it most when mashed in a half-and-half combination with potatoes. The yellow-orange of the rutabaga and the white of the potato blend well. I serve the mash with a couple of fried eggs on top and accompanied by a carrot salad. It's real peasant food, and I love it. You also can turn rutabagas into hash browns or chips if you need to tempt recalcitrant children. Make a point of getting to know this dependable food. You'll be pleasantly surprised.

Plant rutabagas a few weeks after the summer solstice, around the Fourth of July. Choose a spot that has not recently grown another cabbage relative. If you have harvested a patch of early onions or scallions, rutabagas are the perfect succession crop. Mix in some compost or leaf mold before planting and keep the rows moist until they germinate. I plant in rows 16 inches apart and thin the seedlings to 4 to 6 inches in the row. I usually harvest rutabagas later than other root crops because cold is an important ingredient in their flavor. There is no need to wax them, as with the flaccid specimens in the supermarket. They store perfectly in open containers in the root cellar.

SALAD GREENS Mixed species

Planting Distance—

> Arugula: Rows 6 inches apart across bed; seeds 1 inch apart; thin to 6 inches apart.
>
> Claytonia: Rows 8 inches apart across bed; plants 6 inches apart.
>
> Mizuna: Rows 5 inches apart across bed; seeds 1 inch apart; thin to 10 inches apart.
>
> Sorrel: Rows 12 inches apart across bed; plants 12 inches apart.

Crop Rotation—Arugula and mizuna are related to the cabbage family. Claytonia and sorrel are not closely related to any other vegetable crops or to each other.

Growing Tips—Add mature compost to the soil in the winter cold frames.

Storage Tips—These will all keep in covered containers in the refrigerator for a few days, but I encourage you to harvest them fresh daily.

Variety Tips—There are few distinctive varieties, so most catalogs offer these plants by name only.

This category comprises 4 principal crops: arugula, claytonia, mizuna, and sorrel. I group them together because they are probably unfamiliar to many gardeners. If you are one of the unacquainted, give them a try. They are jewels of the winter garden. Once you try them, you will share my enthusiasm.

ARUGULA *(Eruca sativa)* has long been a popular salad crop in Europe. When grown under cool conditions, it has a mild but distinctive flavor. Arugula is often included as an ingredient in mesclun mixes because it does well as a cutting green. I prefer to sow it in single rows so I can mix and match my salad at will. I

Arugula

Claytonia

Mizuna

Sorrel

sow arugula in rows 6 inches apart and place 1 seed per inch. I thin the seedlings progressively to 6 inches apart and then pick single leaves. A late-October planting in a tunnel-covered cold frame will yield through the cold months. I begin making new sowings in the tunnel-covered frames in January, and the thinnings from the new crop are large enough to start picking by late February.

CLAYTONIA *(Montia perfoliata)* should win the winter salad sleeper award for being both unknown and irresistible. Claytonia was originally a native West Coast weed known as miner's lettuce. Recently it has come back across the Atlantic from Holland and Germany, where it was transformed into a popular green called winter purslane. In the United States, it is called claytonia after John Clayton, an early American botanist. Along with mâche, I find it the most delightful of winter salad crops. This almost ornamental plant will keep growing delicious salad leaves all winter in tunnel-covered cold frames. In spring, it becomes twice as beautiful in the salad bowl when small white blossoms appear in the center of each leaf. I sow claytonia seeds in groups of 3 in early September. When the plants are large enough, I transplant them to the covered frames at a 6-inch spacing in 8-inch rows. The leaves grow upward on 4-inch stems. To harvest, I grasp the leaves and cut the stems below them. The plant will keep producing new leaves throughout the winter.

MIZUNA *(Brassica rapa)* is a mild and delicate Oriental plant with a slight mustard flavor. Its deeply cut fringed leaves are as lovely in a salad mix as they are delicious. It will grow to the size of a large lettuce plant and yield over a long period if cut back to encourage new leaf production. I prefer to harvest it at the seedling stage. I sow mizuna in succession in a cold frame during the fall and winter and cut the plants when they are about 3 to 4 inches tall to serve whole in salads. When the plants get larger, I pick individual leaves. Mizuna can be transplanted, but I prefer to sow the seeds directly in 5-inch rows with seeds 1 inch apart. I harvest the small plants as thinnings, then leave single plants at a 10-by-10-inch spacing for later harvest. Fall sowings will yield through the cold months. A January sowing is ready to begin thinning in late February.

Claytonia

SORREL *(Rumex acetosa),* also called garden sorrel, shares the lemon piquancy and tang of the common weed from which it was developed, but it has larger leaves and is much more productive. Sorrel holds a unique place among salad greens because it is a perennial. Only one seeding is necessary. In subsequent years, you just select the plant with the nicest leaves, divide it, and transplant the clumps to the cold frames in the fall. Half a dozen plants spaced 12 inches apart will provide plenty of leaves for salads and classic sorrel soup throughout the entire winter.

The best salads are patterns of mixed greenery. These crops enhance that mix by adding new shapes, textures, and flavors. For fresh salads throughout the winter, you will find arugula, claytonia, mizuna, and sorrel, plus mâche and spinach, to be almost unbelievably productive and dependable without any added heat in tunnel-covered cold frames. These hardy crops are available every day all winter here in Zone 5. Once they are planted, all you do is pick and eat.

These crops also are useful replacements for a winter crop that didn't get planted or didn't germinate. Arugula, claytonia, and mizuna, along with mâche and spinach, will germinate and grow anytime during the winter in tunnel-covered cold frames. Use them to replant any gaps in your winter garden.

A number of other salad ingredients should be mentioned here. Cress, purslane, red mustard, chervil, orach, and plantain are some of the lesser-known possibilities available in specialist seed catalogs. They may fit your growing conditions and salad preferences better than my favorites. I sow them in short rows 4 inches apart and cut them with scissors when they are 4 inches high to use as part of my own mesclun mix. Whichever of these I grow, I have found that a soil amended with mature compost (and limestone where necessary to maintain a pH of 6.5 to 6.8) will grow the tastiest and healthiest specimens.

SORREL See SALAD GREENS

Spinach

SPINACH   *Spinacia oleracea*

Planting Distance—Rows 8 inches apart across row; seeds 1 inch apart; thin to 4 inches.

Crop Rotation—Related to beets and Swiss chard.

Growing Tips—A fertile soil, plenty of moisture, a neutral pH, and cool temperatures will grow the best crop. More resistant to bolting in clay than in sandy soil.

Storage Tips—Will store for a week in the refrigerator but always best eaten fresh.

Variety Tips—Spring • *Tyee*
Fall • *Indian Summer*
Winter • *Winter Bloomsdale*

Spinach is an important contributor to the fall, winter, and spring harvest. This hardy green will germinate and grow at temperatures only slightly above freezing. Spinach is at its best when grown in a well-composted soil. The balanced nutrient release from mature compost makes a difference in its flavor and nutritional value. Spinach grown with excessive nitrogen from imbalanced fertilization has a flat, metallic flavor and often has high levels of nitrates.

The spinach season begins in the fall. In Zone 5, I start planting between August 1 and 15. The first spinach is ready to harvest in September, and the cool temperatures and short fall days keep it in prime condition until hard freezes. I continue planting for continuous harvest according to the schedule on p. 185.

Since young spinach thinnings are a delicious addition to salad green mixtures, I sow the seeds 1 inch apart in rows 8 inches apart and get many salad servings by progressive thinning before the leaves reach cooking size.

During the dog days of summer when spinach goes to seed (especially in my sandy soil), I plan to enjoy other greens until the fall crop begins. Some of those other greens have "spinach" in their name, even though they are not related. New Zealand spinach *(Tetragonia expansa)* and Malabar spinach *(Basella alba)* are excellent warm-weather vegetables for those who wish a spinach-type leafy green. You can grow them on trellises in the mobile tunnel during the summer, since they are vinelike and appreciate the extra heat.

Spinach Planting Dates		
Date	Site	Use
September 15	Cold frame	For late-fall eating.
September 25	Outdoors	For wintering over, cover with straw in late November.
October 1	Cold frame	For wintering over.
October 15	Cold frame under tunnel	For winter consumption.
January 15 to March 1	Cold frame	For an early-spring crop under tunnel.
April 15	Outdoors	For an outdoor spring crop.

SQUASH FAMILY   *Cucurbita* spp.

Planting Distance—
   Winter squash: 1 row per 30-inch-wide bed; plants 30 inches apart.
   Summer squash: 1 row per 30-inch-wide bed; plants 24 inches apart.
Crop Rotation—Related to melons, cucumbers, and pumpkins.
Growing Tips—Dried seaweed added to the soil will improve pest resistance in squash crops.
Storage Tips—Winter squashes store best at 50°F in a fairly dry atmosphere.
Variety Tips—Zucchini • *Zucchini Elite*
   Climbing • *Zucchetta Rampicante*
   Yellow • *Seneca Prolific*
   Winter • *Buttercup*

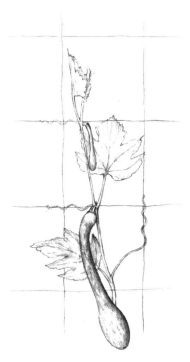

Zucchetta Rampicante
on a trellis.

If you think zucchini has a reputation as an overzealous producer, wait until you meet my favorite summer squash. *Zucchetta Rampicante* is a climbing zucchini that grows fruits on long vines. Its rampant growth makes it suitable for a sci-fi feature titled "The Zucchini That Ate Manhattan." But when something tastes this good, it can do all the growing it wants.
   I train a few *Zucchetta* plants on one of my trellises, where the

long, curved fruits can hang from the vines. The flesh is firmer and not as watery as that of regular zucchini. Both flavor and texture are superb when the squash is cooked alone or in any standard recipe.

My favorite winter squash, *Buttercup,* and most of its relatives are also vine crops. They are the one common vegetable that doesn't fit neatly into the spacing of my 30-inch-wide beds. Pumpkins wouldn't fit either, but I don't grow them, since I think *Buttercup* makes a better "pumpkin" pie. My solution to long vines is to grow them at the edge of the garden and encourage the vines to run through the fence and out onto the lawn. I suppose I could train them up a trellis, but I don't have additional trellis space. Their forays outside the garden confines have not been a problem. Once the first fall frost nips the vines, I harvest the fruits and drag the vines to the compost heap.

I have always cured winter squashes to harden the skin before storage by leaving them on a sunny porch for a few weeks and providing frost protection when necessary. According to the latest information from the storage experts, that step is not necessary. I know that curing is not required for the acorn and delicata types, which are *Cucurbita pepo.* But for the other winter squashes, most of which are *Cucurbita maxima,* I plan to keep curing them as I always have. I am reluctant to give up a system that has served me well. I also think they look pretty on the porch.

The entire squash family, including the bush-type summer squash and zucchini, grow well in soil amended with compost. They germinate best in a warm soil. For an extra-early harvest, you may wish to start them about 3 weeks ahead and transplant the seedlings after the danger of frost has passed. I sow a few zucchini seeds on May 21, June 21, and July 21. I recommend succession planting to keep zucchini in line. I can remove the large plants from the previous sowing and put them on the compost heap once the new plants start to bear. Older, overgrown zucchini plants tend to take over the garden paths, making it harder to move about. They also are more likely to hide their fruits. The younger plants are more productive and the fruits easier to pick.

SWISS CHARD   *Beta vulgaris cicla*

Planting Distance—3 rows per 30-inch-wide bed; plants 10
  inches apart.
Crop Rotation—Related to beets and spinach.
Growing Tips—Occasional top dressing with compost will
  maintain production.
Storage Tips—Eat fresh.
Variety Tips—Hardiest • *Argentata*
  Red-leaved • *Charlotte*

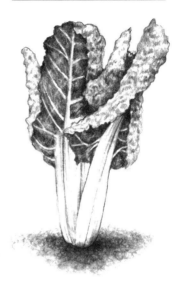

Swiss chard

Swiss chard is a beautiful, dependable, and underappreciated
vegetable. I originally attributed the lack of fans to its undis-
tinguished name: Switzerland is not the culinary capital of the
world, and chard (from the French *chardon,* "thistle") adds little
additional appeal. In England, a common name for chard is
perpetual spinach, a term that would likely inhibit generations of
children from ever trying it at all. However, its French name,
poirée, makes it sound and taste delicious.

You harvest chard over a long period by picking leaves as they
reach the desired size, leaving the heart of the plant to continue
producing more. Both the protected growing conditions in the
cool months and the selective harvesting result in a tender,
higher-quality leaf. When chard is grown during the outdoor
season, the hot summer climate toughens the leaves. The outdoor
grower can achieve more tender leaves by treating chard like
beets—making succession plantings and harvesting the whole
plant when the size of baby beets and greens.

When grown under the protection of a cold frame or greenhouse, chard is a reliable winter producer. If the seeds are sown
in July and the seedlings transplanted to a cold frame in August,
chard will produce dependably from October to May. When
grown in outdoor, unprotected conditions, chard is hardy enough
to keep growing new leaves quite late into the fall. Even in the
coldest parts of New England, I have noticed that frozen chard
plants in the outdoor garden will come right back during the first
midwinter thaw, although they will usually succumb to the next
onslaught of cold.

The same growing tips that apply to beets also apply to chard,
as they are close relatives. When treated as a long-season, cut-

and-come-again crop, chard needs some extra care. I have always found an occasional top dressing of compost to be a tonic for keeping long-season chard tender and tasty. Chard can be transplanted or direct-seeded. I sow chard as a transplant crop and set out seedlings in the garden 3 weeks later. For whole-plant harvest, I direct-seed chard in 10-inch rows and thin the plants to 4 inches apart. For long-season production, I transplant the seedlings at a 10-by-10-inch spacing. A bed of well-grown chard, especially the red-leaved varieties, is as decorative as it is delicious. Try chard in any dish where you might use other greens. You won't be disappointed.

TOMATO *Lycopersicon esculentum*

Planting Distance—
   Trellis: 1 row per 30-inch-wide bed; plants 15 inches apart.
   Ground: 1 row per 30-inch-wide bed; plants 30 inches apart.
*Crop Rotation—*Related to potatoes, peppers, and eggplant.
*Growing Tips—*Use a weekly spray of compost tea to enhance plant vigor.
*Storage Tips—*I think drying beats any other tomato preservation method I have tried.
*Variety Tips—*Early • *Oregon Spring*
   Ground • *Valley Girl*
   Cherry • *Ruby Pearl, Sweet 100+*
   Trellis • *Carmello, Dona*
   Drying • *Principe Borghese*

Tomato

   If nothing else can compel you to begin a garden, let me suggest the desire to eat a *real* tomato. In this case, "real" means a tomato bred for eating, not shipping; grown in a fully fertile, humus-rich soil; and picked at the peak of its ripeness and flavor. Normal tomatoes are a delightful treat; when above average, they are exceptional; when truly well grown, they are beyond belief. Henry David Thoreau said he wanted to live deliberately so as not to come to the end of life and find he had never lived. The tomato lover says you want to grow your own so as not to come to the end of life and find you have never tasted a real tomato.

   When the commercial catalogs praise the flavor of a tomato variety, they mean that despite being picked green, gassed to make it turn red, and shipped to a faraway location, its taste is not totally insipid. The tomato flavor of commercial-industrial specimens is best represented by a flat line at the bottom of the graph. Real tomato flavor is a bell curve, barely on the graph if picked green, then ascending through layers of soil fertility, variety selection, cultural technique, sun, and warmth to a crescendo that is maintained briefly before descending on the other side.

How do you create such delights? Compost, sunshine, and patience are the 3 main ingredients. But let's start at the beginning. The best tomato transplants for your garden are 6 to 7 weeks old, each in a 4-inch pot. A 4-inch pot? Absolutely. You want plenty of room to encourage a strong root system and plenty of potting soil to feed the young plant. The six-pack of tomatoes sold at the garden center has less soil than is ideal for a single plant. Those plants will eventually produce tomatoes, but never as dependably as you will with good plants.

If you are growing plants at home, start them 6 to 7 weeks before the outdoor transplant date. Keep the newly sown flats warm (70° to 80°F) until they germinate. At 10 days, move the seedlings to a wider spacing (about 2 by 2 inches). Don't wait until they get bigger before you move them. It is precisely those crowded conditions that are inhibiting their growth. Another 10 days to 2 weeks later, move them to 4-inch pots. Try to maintain 70°F daytime and 60°F nighttime temperatures throughout the process.

Set the pots in your sunniest window. When the leaves begin to touch, space them farther apart. Move them to a cold frame or tunnel for the last 10 days. Provide a little heat if you can. By the time they are 7 weeks old, you will have sturdy, well-rooted plants with the first flower clusters ready to open. If your growing conditions are cooler, they will take a little longer.

If you use the standard potting mix suggested in Chapter 5, you won't need to feed the plants. There is adequate nutrition in the mix to carry the tomatoes until they are transplanted. If for some reason the plants look hungry (poor color, stunted growth), use a compost tea or one of the liquid seaweed-fish products as an effective temporary food.

When they are ready for the garden, I set the plants at 15 inches apart in a single row if I plan to trellis them. That requires

10 to 12 plants for a 15-foot bed. I space them 30 inches apart if they are to be grown on the ground. A total of 12 to 24 plants will supply me with both fresh eating and drying tomatoes. If you want to give the plants a boost at setting-out time, fill the planting holes with the same dilution of compost tea or seaweed-fish emulsion used earlier and let it soak into the soil before setting out the plants.

The description in the seed catalog will tell you whether your tomatoes are determinate or indeterminate. The determinate varieties are best grown on the ground or in low cages because they don't grow much after the fruits form. *Oregon Spring, Valley Girl,* and *Principe Borghese* are determinate. Indeterminate varieties such as *Ruby Pearl, Sweet 100+, Carmello,* and *Dona* are suitable for trellis culture, as they continue to grow and ripen fruits simultaneously.

I prefer to grow my fresh tomatoes on a trellis. Trellised tomatoes are not only twice as productive and form a beautiful red and green vertical hedge, but they also ripen up to 2 weeks earlier and are less prone to rot, since the fruits have no contact with the soil.

I prune my plants to one stem by removing all the suckers that sprout between the main stem and the leaf branches. Pruning is a simple process that I attend to once a week. The plants are supported by a length of 4- to 5-ply untreated garden twine, which I tie to the trellis crossbar at the top and to a garden stake at the bottom. I wind the string gently around the stem as the plant grows upward. When the plants reach the top of the trellis, I cut them off at a height of one branch above the highest fruit cluster. I prune leaves from tomato plants if they are looking ragged, but I prefer to leave them if they are healthy. Either way, I never remove leaves above the lowest cluster of ripening fruits.

If growing conditions are less than ideal, you can help the plants by pruning off extra fruits. Remove some of the tomatoes (the smallest) from the first two clusters at the bottom of the plant. Three to four fruits per cluster are enough to leave on the *Beefsteak*-type plants. By thinning the fruits you decrease early stress on the plants and allow more energy for rooting.

If your garden has been troubled by tomato blight, I recommend spraying the foliage once a week with compost tea. European studies have found a tea made from soaking well-decomposed compost in water for 4 days to be a very effective treatment for strengthening the plant's resistance to blight. Adding seaweed to the soil also is effective.

Don't mulch your tomato plants until both the weather and the soil have warmed up. Whereas early mulching will cool the soil and slow them down, later mulching will help retain moisture for the rest of the summer.

One final note on the proper pronunciation of the name. When speaking of the mediocre, run-of-the-mill, commercial-industrial tomato, I happily call it a *tom AY toe*. But when speaking of a compost-fertilized, sun-ripened, full-flavored, homegrown beauty, the proper pronunciation is definitely *tom AHH toe,* with the emphasis on the *AHH!*

First Fall Frost Dates for All Regions of the United States

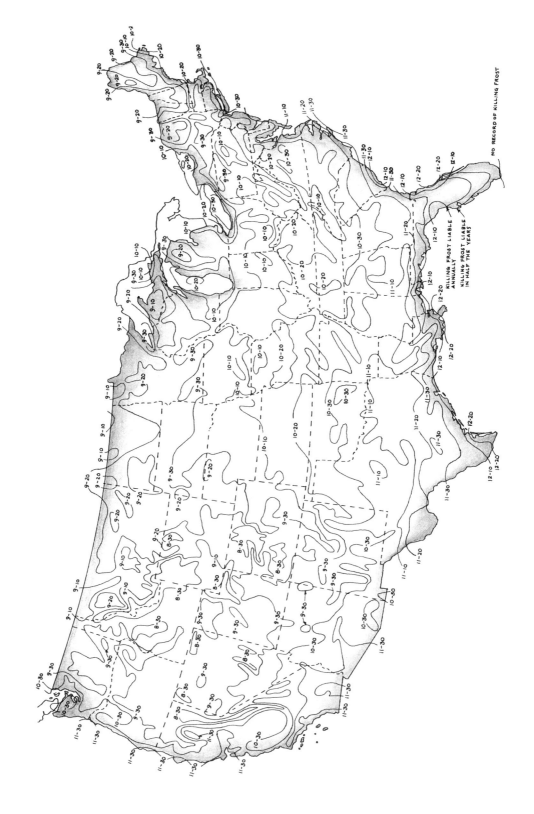

Credit: USDA

TABLE 14

Planting Dates for an Extended Harvest

The table on the following pages is compiled from USDA information with modifications based on my experience. The dates given indicate when you can safely plant vegetables in the open for a late-season harvest, for all sections of the country.

You can adapt these tables for cold frame and tunnel planting. First find the column for the approximate first fall frost date for your area. (Find the date on the USDA map nearest to the place you live if you are unsure of your frost dates.) Then read 2 or 3 columns to the right of this date for when to plant in the cold frame, and 4 to 5 columns to the right for when to plant in the tunnel-protected cold frames.

These dates are your quidelines. They are subject to the variability of local conditions but will give you a place to start. Your experience and observations will be needed to refine this general information into a planting schedule for your specific garden climate.

Crop	Aug. 30	Sept 10	Sept 20	Sept. 30	Oct. 10	Oct. 20
Asparagus					10/20-11/15	11/1-12/15
Bean	5/15-6/15	6/1-7/1	6/1-7/1	6/1-7/10	6/15-7/20	7/1-8/1
Beet	5/15-6/15	ditto	ditto	ditto	6/15-7/20	7/1-8/5
Broccoli, Sprouts	5/1-6/1	5/1-6/1	5/1-6/15	6/1-6/30	ditto	7/1-8/1
Cabbage	ditto	ditto	ditto	6/1-7/10	6/1-7/15	7/1-7/20
Cabbage, Chinese	5/15-6/15	5/15-6/15	6/1-7/1	6/1-7/15	6/15-8/1	7/15-7/15
Carrot	ditto	ditto	5/1-8/1	6/1-8/1	6/1-8/1	7/15-8/15
Cauliflower	5/1-6/1	5/1-7/1	5/1-7/1	5/10-7/15	6/1-7/25	7/1-8/5
Celery, Celeriac	ditto	5/15-6/15	5/15-7/1	6/1-7/5	6/1-7/15	7/1-8/1
Chard	5/15-6/15	5/15-7/1	6/1-7/1	ditto	6/1-7/20	ditto
Chicory, witloof	5/15-6/15	5/15-6/15	ditto	6/1-7/1	6/1-7/1	6/15-7/15
Chicory, green	6/1-6/15	6/1-7/1	6/1-7/1	6/15-7/15	7/1-8/1	7/15-8/15
Cornsalad (mâche)	ditto	5/15-7/1	6/15-8/1	7/15-9/1	8/15-9/15	9/1-10/15
Corn		6/1-7/1	6/1-7/1	6/1-7/10	6/1-7/20	
Claytonia	6/15-7/1	6/15-8/1	7/15-9/1	8/15-9/15	8/15-9/15	9/1-10/1
Cucumber		6/1-6/15	6/1-7/1	6/1-7/16	6/1-7/1	6/1-7/15
Dandelion	6/1-6/15	6/1-7/1	6/1-7/1	6/1-8/1	7/15-9/1	8/1-9/15
Eggplant				5/30-6/10	5/15-6/15	6/1-7/1
Endive, Escarole	6/1-7/1	6/1-7/1	6/15-7/15	6/15-8/1	7/1-8/15	7/15-9/1
Garlic	10/10	10/10	10/15	10/15	10/20	10/30
Kale	5/15-6/15	5/15-6/15	6/1-7/1	6/15-7/15	7/1-8/1	7/15-8/15
Kohlrabi	ditto	6/1-7/1	6/1-7/15	ditto	ditto	ditto
Leek	5/1-6/1	5/1-6/1	5/1-6/15	5/1-6/15	5/1-6/15	6/1-7/1
Lettuce	5/15-7/15	5/15-7/15	6/1-8/1	6/1-8/1	7/15-9/1	7/30-9/10
Melon			5/1-6/15	5/15-6/1	6/1-6/15	6/15-7/20
Mizuna	5/15-7/15	5/15-6/1	6/1-8/1	6/15-8/1	7/15-8/15	8/1-9/1
Onion, bulb	5/1-6/10	5/1-6/10				
Onion, green	5/1-6/1	5/1-6/10	6/15-7/15	6/15-8/1	7/15-8/15	7/15-9/1
Parsley, Parsley root	5/15-6/15	5/1-6/15	6/1-7/1	6/1-7/15	6/15-8/1	7/15-8/15
Parsnip	5/15-6/1	ditto	5/15-6/15	6/1-7/1	6/1-6/10	
Peas	5/10-6/15	5/1-7/1	6/1-7/15	6/1-8/1		
Pepper			6/1-6/20	6/1-7/1	6/1-7/1	6/1-7/10
Potato	5/15-6/1	5/1-6/15	5/1-6/15	5/1-6/15	5/15-6/15	6/15-7/15
Radicchio	9/1-10/1	9/15-10-15	9/15-10/1	10/1-11/1	10/15-11/15	10/15-11/1
Radish	5/1-7/15	5/1-8/1	6/1-8/15	7/1-9/1	7/15-9/15	8/1-10/1
Rutabaga	5/15-6/15	5/1-6/15	6/1-7/1	6/1-7/1	6/15-7/15	7/10-7/20
Salsify	5/15-6/1	5/10-6/10	5/20-6/20	6/1-6/20	6/1-7/1	6/1-7/1
Sorrel	5/15-6/15	5/1-6/15	6/1-7/1	6/1-7/15	7/1-8/1	7/15-8/15
Spinach	5/15-6/1	6/1-7/15	6/1-8/1	7/1-8/15	8/1-9/1	8/1-9/1
Spinach, New Zealand				5/15-7/1	6/1-7/15	6/1-8/1
Squash, summer	6/10-6/20	6/1-6/20	5/15-7/1	6/1-7/1	ditto	6/1-7/20
Squash, winter			5/20-6/10	6/1-6/15	6/1-7/1	6/1-7/1
Tomato	6/20-6/30	6/10-6/20	6/1-6/20	6/1-6/20	6/1-6/20	6/1-7/1
Turnip	5/15-6/15	6/1-7/1	6/1-7/15	6/1-8/1	7/1-8/1	7/15-8/15

Crop	Oct. 30	Nov. 10	Nov 20	Nov. 30	Dec. 10	Dec. 20
Asparagus	11/15-1/1	12/1-1/1				
Bean	7/1-8/15	7/1-9/1	7/1-9/10	8/15-9/20	9/1-9/30	9/1-11/1
Beet	8/1-9/1	8/1-10/1	9/1-12/1	9/1-12/15	9/1-12/31	9/1-12/31
Broccoli, Sprouts	7/1-8/15	8/1-9/1	8/1-9/15	8/1-10/1	8/1-11/1	ditto
Cabbage	8/1-9/1	9/1-9/15	9/1-12/1	9/1-12/31	9/1-12/31	ditto
Cabbage, Chinese	8/1-9/15	8/15-10/1	9/1-10/15	9/1-11/1	9/1-11/15	9/1-12/1
Carrot	7/1-8/15	8/1-9/1	9/1-11/1	9/15-12/1	9/15-12/1	9/15-12/1
Cauliflower	7/15-8/15	ditto	8/1-9/15	8/15-10/10	9/1-10/20	9/15-11/1
Celery, Celeriac	6/15-8/15	7/1-8/15	7/15-9/1	8/1-12/1	9/1-12/31	10/1-12/31
Chard	6/1-9/10	6/1-9/15	6/1-10/1	6/1-11/1	6/1-12/1	6/1-12/31
Chicory, witloof	7/1-8/10	7/10-8/20	7/20-9/1	8/15-9/30	8/15-10/15	8/15-10/15
Chicory, green	8/1-9/15	8/15-10/1	8/25-11/1	9/1-12/1	9/1-12/31	9/1-12/31
Cornsalad (mache)	9/15-11/1	10/1-12/1	10/1-12/1	10/1-12/31	10/1-12/31	10/1-12/31
Corn	6/1-8/1	6/1-8/15	6/1-9/1			
Claytonia	9/15-10/15	10/1-11/1	10/1-11/10	10/1-11/20	10/1-12/31	10/1-12/31
Cucumber	6/1-8/1	6/1-8/15	6/1-8/15	7/15-9/15	8/15-10/1	8/15-10/1
Dandelion	8/15-10/1	9/1-10/15	9/1-11/1	9/15-12/15	10/1-12/31	10/1-12-31
Eggplant	6/1-7/1	6/1-7/15	6/1-8/1	7/1-9/1	8/1-9/30	8/1-9/30
Endive, Escarole	7/15-8/15	8/1-9/1	9/1-10/1	9/1-11/15	9/1-12/31	9/1-12/31
Garlic	10/30	8/1-10/1	8/15-10/1	9/1-11/15	9/15-11/15	9/15-11/15
Kale	7/15-9/1	8/1-9/15	8/15-10/15	9/1-12/1	9/1-12/31	9/1-12/31
Kohlrabi	8/1-9/1	8/15-9/15	9/1-10/15	ditto	9/15-12/31	ditto
Leek	7/1-8/1	8/1-8/15	9/1-11/1	9/1-11/1	9/1-11/1	9/15-11/1
Lettuce	8/15-10	8/25-10/1	9/1-11/1	9/1-12/1	9/15-12/31	9/15-12/31
Melon	7/1-7/15	7/15-7/30				
Mizuna	8/15-10/15	8/15-11/1	9/1-12/1	9/1-12/1	9/1-12/1	9/15-12/1
Onion, bulb		9/1-10/15	10/1-12/31	10/1-12/31	10/1-12/31	10/1-12/31
Onion, green	8/1-10/15	8/1-10/15	9/1-11/1	9/1-11/1	9/1-11/1	9/15-11/1
Parsley, Parsley root	8/1-9/15	9/1-11/15	9/1-12/31	9/1-12/31	9/15-12/31	9/1-12/31
Parsnip			8/1-9/1	9/1-11/15	9/1-12/1	9/1-12/1
Peas	8/1-9/15	9/1-11/1	10/1-12/1	10/1-12/31	10/1-12/31	10/1-12/31
Pepper	6/1-7/20	6/1-8/1	6/1-8/15	6/15-9/1	8/15-10/1	8/15-10/1
Potato	7/20-8/10	7/25-8/20	8/10-9/15	8/1-9/15	8/1-9/15	8/1-9/15
Radicchio	11/1-12/1					
Radish	8/15-10/15	9/1-11/15	9/1-12/1	9/1-12/31	8/1-9/15	10/1-12/31
Rutabaga	7/15-8/1	7/15-8/15	8/1-9/1	9/1-11/15	10/1-11/15	10/15-11/15
Salsify	6/1-7/10	6/15-7/20	7/15-8/15	8/15-9/30	8/15-10/15	9/1-10/31
Sorrel	8/1-9/15	8/15-10/1	8/15-10/15	9/1-11/15	9/1-12/15	9/1-12/31
Spinach	9/1-10/1	9/15-11/1	10/1-12/1	10/1-12/31	10/1-12/31	10/1-12/31
Spinach, New Zealand	6/1-8/1	6/1-8/15	6/1-8/15			
Squash, summer	ditto	6/1-8/10	6/1-8/20	6/1-9/1	6/1-9/15	6/1-10/1
Squash, winter	6/10-7/10	6/20-7/20	7/1-8/1	7/15-8/15	8/1-9/1	8/1-9/1
Tomato	6/1-7/1	6/1-7/15	6/1-8/1	8/1-9/1	8/15-10/1	9/1-11/1
Turnip	8/1-9/15	9/1-10/15	9/1-11/15	9/1-11/15	10/1-12/1	10/1-12/31

FROST ZONE MAP OF THE UNITED STATES AND CANADA

Credit: adapted from the USDA

GARDEN TOOLS AND SUPPLIES
AND THEIR SOURCES

I list the sources from which I purchase supplies for use in my garden. I am familiar with these firms, and I know that they stocked these items at the time of publication. This is not meant to be an endorsement of the companies mentioned or an exclusion of other suppliers not listed.

Compost and Soil Amendments

The *Biostack* backyard **compost container** is sold by:

Smith and Hawken
25 Corte Madera
Mill Valley, CA 94941
(415) 383-2000

A comparable model, the *Soilsaver*, is sold by:

Lee Valley Tools, Ltd.
1080 Morrison Drive
Ottawa, Ontario
Canada K2H 8K7

Both companies also sell a **compost thermometer** to help you keep track of heap temperature.

A nice-looking wooden slat composter called the *BioBin* is sold by:

W. Altee Burpee & Co.
300 Park Ave.
Warminster, PA 18974
(215) 674-4170

If phosphate rock, greensand, dried blood, seaweed-fish emulsion and other **soil amendments** are not available at your local garden center, you can purchase them by mail from the companies listed below. These companies also offer a wide selection of other products.

Necessary Trading Company
One Nature's Way
New Castle, VA 24127
(703) 864-5103

Peaceful Valley Farm Supply
P.O. Box 2209
Grass Valley, CA 95945
(916) 272-4769

Nutrite, Inc.
P.O. Box 160
Elmira, Ontario
Canada N3B 2Z6
(519) 669-5401

Mountain Station Holdings, Ltd.
P.O. Box 430
Kimberly, British Columbia
Canada BC V1A 2Y9
(604) 489-4717

Tillers

In both my professional market garden career and my home garden, I have been pleased with the quality of rotary tillers from Mainline, Inc. They are well-built and dependable.

Mainline of North America, Inc.
P.O. Box 526
London, OH 43140

Seeds

I purchase most of my seeds from the following seed catalogs. They carry a good selection of conventional and unconventional crops, they offer varieties with exceptional flavor, and they introduce enough new products every year to keep me intrigued.

Johnny's Selected Seeds
Foss Hill Road
Albion, ME 04910
(207) 437-4301

The Cook's Garden
P.O. Box 535
Londonderry, VT 05148
(802) 824-3400

Shepherd's Garden Seeds
30 Irene Street
Torrington, CT 06790
(203) 482-3638

Some of my favorite varieties are available only from specific catalogs. I look to these other fine catalogs when I want seeds for:

Bergkabis cabbage—Vesey's Seeds Ltd., P.O. Box 9000, Calais, ME 04619 (902) 892-1048
In Canada: P.O. Box 9000, Charlottestown, Prince Edward Island, PEI 1P0 (902) 892-1048

Chieftan Savoy cabbage—Stokes Seeds, P.O. Box 548, Buffalo, NY 14240 (716) 672-8844.

In Canada: P.O. Box 10, St. Catherine's, Ontario, L2R 6R6 (416) 688-4300

Gigante kohlrabi—Nichols Garden Nursery, 1190 North Pacific Highway, Albany, OR 97321 (503) 928-9280

Gold Star melon—Harris Seeds, 60 Saginaw Drive, P.O. Box 22960, Rochester, NY 14692 (716) 442-0410

Grande Beurre artichoke—Thompson and Morgan Inc., P.O. Box 1308, Jackson, NJ 08527 (908) 363-2225

Seed potatoes in every color, size, and maturity range imaginable are available from: Ronniger's Seed Potatoes, Star Route, Moyie Springs, ID 83845.

In Canada, order seed potatoes from: Becker's Seed Potatoes, RR#1, Trout Creek, Ontario POH 2L0.

Both Johnny's Selected Seeds and Peaceful Valley Farm Supply are good sources for seeds of the many **green manures**. Your local garden or farm supply store may also stock many of them.

Garden Tools

In the course of working with Smith and Hawken as a garden tool consultant, I have encouraged them to carry my favorite tools. Request their *Tools of the Trade* catalog.

1. European-style **scythe**. They also sell *The Scythe Book*, by David Tresemer, which will teach you how to use and enjoy using a scythe for mowing grass and weeds.
2. **Curved-tine cultivator**
3. **Broadfork**
4. **Right-Angle trowel**
5. A **grading rake** with nylon teeth that is the perfect size for smoothing my 30-inch-wide beds. It is also an excellent design for raking up the compost material that you mow with the scythe.

6. **Collineal hoe**
7. **Stirrup or oscillating hoe**
8. A wide range of **watering cans** and watering wands with the fine rose that makes a gentle spray for seedlings.
9. Hose connectors, **sprinklers**, and timers to make your watering easier.

In Canada, a similar selection of tools is available from Lee Valley Tools, Inc.

The **trellis netting** I use is available from Johnny's Selected Seeds. The **spray emitters** for irrigating your cold frames are carried by most greenhouse supply companies. (Consult your Yellow Pages.) The **natural wood preservative** I use is called *Donnos*. It is one of a line of natural products distributed by:

Eco Design Company
1365 Rufina Circle
Santa Fe, NM 87501
(505) 438-3448

Natural wood preservatives are also available from:

Livos Canada
P.O. Box 220, Station A
Fredericton, New Brunswick
Canada E3B 4Y9
(506) 366-3529

Frames and Tunnels

The **glass substitutes**, *Polygal* and *Lexan*, for glazing the lights of your cold frames are made in a variety of thicknesses by the following companies. ⅛-¼" should be adequate for the Dutch light model. You can contact the following companies for the name of your nearest dealer.

Polygal— Polygal USA, P.O. Box 1567, Janesville, WI 53547
(800) 537-0095

Lexan— General Electric Plastics, One Plastics Avenue, Pittsfield, MA 01201 (800) 451-3147

I am familiar with 2 brands of **temperature-activated automatic venting arms**, the *Thermofor* and the *Solarvent*. They are available from:

Thermofor— Bramen Company, P.O. Box 70, Salem, MA 01970 (508) 745-7765

Solarvent— Dalen Products, Inc. 11110 Gilbert Drive, Knoxville, TN 37922 (615) 966-3256

Dalen also makes a reasonably priced **cold frame**, the *Vent O' Matic III*. It has a built-in automatic venting arm and is ingeniously designed to allow maximum light to reach the plants.

Even more reasonably priced and with vent holes cleverly incorporated into the plastic cover is the *Melbourne Frame*. It comes in a 30- and 48-inch width, both of which are 5 feet long. These frames can be used individually, or, with the end panels removed, they can be set end to end to cover as long a garden bed as you wish. Three of the 30-inch frames cover one of my 30-inch by 15-foot beds. They can be used under the tunnel in winter and as season extenders for the outdoor garden in spring and fall. With the ends removed, they can be stacked and stored in minimal space for the summer months. The *Melbourne Frame* is available from Smith and Hawken.

A wide selection of the **floating covers** used as season extenders and pest barriers, plus the **infrared-transmitting plastic mulch**, are available from Johnny's Selected Seeds and Peaceful Valley Farm Supply.

My simple **hoop-style tunnel greenhouse** is an easily-erected model available in 12-,14-, and 17-foot widths from:

X.S. Smith
Drawer X
Red Bank, NJ 07701
(908) 222-4600

Greenhouse plastic can be purchased through your local greenhouse supply company. You will save money if you buy a 100-foot roll. Since the plastic lasts 3 years in use, a 100-foot roll will provide enough to cover your tunnel for 6 to 9 years, depending on tunnel size and how much you use for the ends. If you calculate your cost per year as the total cost of the plastic divided by the years of service, you will see that the greenhouse covering is a minimal expense considering the value of the food to be harvested. **Fiberglass rods** for the instant tunnel can usually be located by calling the listings under "Fiberglass Products" in the Yellow Pages. Plans for homemade **wooden greenhouses** can be purchased from:

The Department of Natural Resources, Management and
    Engineering
University of Connecticut
1376 Storrs Road
Storrs, CT 06269

Food Dryer

My **food dryer** is a top-of-the-line *Gardenmaster II* which I purchased from Johnny's Selected Seeds. I highly recommend it. The dried tomatoes alone are worth the price. Addresses for plans to make your own dryer are available from The Department of Natural Resources, Management, and Engineering at the University of Connecticut.

In Canada, write to the following for plans:

Brace Research Inst.
Publications Dept.
Faculty of Engineering
P.O. Box 900
Macdonald College of McGill University
Ste. Anne de Bellvue, Québec
Canada H9X ICO.

ANNOTATED BIBLIOGRAPHY

Garden Books

The New Organic Grower (see below) has an extensive bibliography on the subject of organic gardening. Many of the best old books are out of print. Your local library should be able to find you a copy of any book through interlibrary loan.

Bruce, M.E. *Common Sense Compost Making.* London: Faber and Faber, 1946. This was the first composting book I read and I still find it enjoyable, helpful, and delightfully eccentric.

Coleman, Eliot. *The New Organic Grower.* Chelsea, VT: Chelsea Green, 1989. Gardeners looking for more in-depth explanations of the soil fertility and garden management practices of *The Four-Season Harvest*, plus technical details on tools and greenhouses, will find them in my earlier book.

Damrosch, Barbara. *The Garden Primer.* New York: Workman, 1988. The best general gardening book for beginners and experienced gardeners alike. Everything you could ever want to know is here. The explanations are clear and engagingly written.

Easey, Ben. *Practical Organic Gardening.* London: Faber and Faber, 1955. One of the most comprehensive and reasonable explanations of the ideas and techniques involved in organic gardening.

Nearing, Helen and Scott. *Our Sun-Heated Greenhouse.* Charlotte, VT: Garden Way, 1977. Helen and Scott Nearing have been my neighbors, friends, and teachers since I moved to Maine. Seeing their greenhouse years ago inspired me to investigate the possibilities of harvesting fresh food year-round.

O'Brien, Dalziel. *Intensive Gardening.* London: Faber and Faber, 1956. This book has been a source of ideas for many organic gardeners. Although the author was a commercial grower, her simple and innovative organic methods are applicable anywhere. She provides thorough background material on Dutch lights, composting, and shallow cultivation.

Rodale, J. I. *How to Grow Vegetables and Fruits by the Organic Method.* Emmaus, PA: Rodale Press, 1960. This is the first book I started with many years ago, and I found it very helpful. Good information is timeless.

Salter, P. J., J. K. A. Bleasdale, et al. *Know and Grow Vegetables.* Vols 1 and 2. New York: Oxford University Press, 1979, 1982. Two extremely useful books from the staff of the British National Vegetable Research Station.

Cookbooks

Madison, Deborah. *The Greens Cookbook.* New York: Bantam Books, 1987. When you harvest fresh, homegrown vegetables year-round, you have the best ingredients. Use them to appreciate wonderful recipes. This book does gourmet justice to the high level of quality and variety your garden has produced.

Morash, Marion. *The Victory Garden Cookbook.* New York: Alfred A. Knopf, 1982. If you are wondering how imaginative you can be with both the common and less common winter vegetables, this is the book to consult. It includes delicious recipes from a very talented garden chef, using every vegetable under the sun.

INDEX